HEALING
ON THE
EDGE *of* NOW

A PRACTICAL GUIDE FOR THE USE OF
PSYCHONEUROIMMUNOLOGY

SunShine Press Publications
Hygiene, Colorado

CARL BRAHE

SunShine Press Publications
PO Box 333
Hygiene, Colorado 80533

Cover Design by Robert Schram
Cover Art by Susanna Reynolds
Book Design by Jack Hofer

Publisher's Cataloging-in-Publication Data

Brahe, Carl.
    Healing on the edge of now: a practical guide for the use of
psychoneuroimmunology / Carl Brahe.
    p. cm.
    Includes bibliographical references and index.
    ISBN: 0-9615743-2-1
    1. Psychoneuroimmunology. 2. Mind and body.
3. Alternative medicine. 4. Self-care, Health. I. Title.
RZ401.B81 1992   92-80669
615.851—dc20

Printed in the United States of America
96 95 94 93 5 4 3 2

Dedication

This book is dedicated to Sherry Pennypacker who showed me that life can be full and rich when you are facing death and to Maria Kamakele who convinced me to specialize in psychoneuroimmunology. This book is also dedicated to Spunky and the group who demonstrated how easy healing can be on the edge of now.

The exercises in this book are not intended to replace appropriate professional treatment of your life challenge. This book is offered to guide you in your healing process using all appropriate resources.

Acknowledgments

I wish to express my sincere appreciation to Jack Hofer for his patience and dedication in helping me take these subtle, experiental concepts and translating them into a useful and practical book.

I would also like to thank Anna Brahe, Gretchen Hofer and Glenda Schoonmaker for their great work in editing this book.

I want to thank the following people who's verbal and written teachings made this book possible: Sarasvati Buhrman, Chardin Bersto, Don Campbell, Barbara Carter, Deepak Chopra, Ken Cohen, Dee Coulter, Larry Dossey, Kathryn Fentress, Tom Fox, Robbie Gass, Christina and Stanislov Grof, Micheal Herrick, Evan Hodkins, Pamela and Jeff Krock, Gladys Kuoksa, Ron Kurtz, Ondrea and Stephen Levine, Shar Lew, John McCauley, Janet Mentgen, Gary Mueller, Stephanie Mines, Donna Montei, James Pennebaker, Karen Peterson, Clyde Reid, Laurie Rugenstein, Bernie Siegal, Richard Shane, Holly Smith, Shanna Stanberry, Linda Tharp, Wind Woman, Anna Wise and Fred Young.

Contents

Exercises

There is no such thing as a problem without a gift for you in its hands.
—Richard Bach, *Illusions*

Preface

Where is your awareness right now? Part of your awareness is present with reading and processing these words. You also may be aware of other thoughts and sensations. What percentage is aware of the past or future? What percentage is here in the moment?

A part of your awareness may be used in thinking about something that happened earlier today, yesterday, in the distant past, or another part might be daydreaming of the future as you read these words.

In our fast-paced lives, we often find it difficult to be present for more than a few moments. We use a variety of strategies to find safety in a sometimes impossible world. To find that safety, our strategies seem to involve creating an illusion of not existing in the here and now where it might be dangerous to our egos, emotions or bodies. A main strategy for safety is like a hold over from our early learning of peek-a-boo. On a certain level of our consciousness we believe that if we distract ourselves from being present in the moment, we become invisible and therefore safe. By tricking ourselves that way, we bring into the moment the thoughts and elements that we use for distracting ourselves. By investing our awareness in our thoughts and daydreams, we create and maintain safety in the moment. This can be a blessing or a nightmare depending on what we choose to think about.

In a story about the Buddha the people asked him what made him the Buddha, "Are you an angel?" they asked. "No," replied the Buddha. "Are you a god then?" they asked. "No," he replied, "I am simply awake." In Ayurveda, the system of medicine native to India, the practitioners believe true healing is awakening to the essence of your true self which is a divine (universal) being.

Turn thy sight unto thyself, that thou mayest find Me standing within thee, mighty, powerful and self-subsisting.
—Bahá'u'lláh, *The Hidden Words*

If each person who reads this book can awaken to the essence of their life energy, the book has succeeded in its mission. The emphasis is on guiding you to experience this essence firsthand. You will learn how to use your life energy to heal and create in the world. I want to stress that I am not implying anyone can heal every disease and ailment. Mystics, gurus, medicine men, medicine women and other healers get the same diseases as everyone else.

The following is an adaptation of a story by Idries Shah. A young man begged of his old teacher, "Please, teach me the most great name of Allah, the word that when said brings unimaginable power. You must teach me so I can serve people."

The old man replied that he might be persuaded to teach the young man the name, but first he must do something. He must sit outside the gates of the city and observe everything that happens for an entire day.

After watching the city gates from a hidden place, the young man returned the next night. The old man asked of him what he had seen.

"Just about dusk," he replied, "an ancient man came to the gate with his back bent beneath a large load of firewood which he was bringing to town to sell. The guard told him to pay a tax to enter the city with his goods. The old man lacked money and the guard not only refused to let him enter the city; he beat him terribly and stole his firewood."

"And if you had known the most great name of Allah, it would have been different?" asked the old man.

"Yes, of course!" exclaimed the young man, "I would have saved that old man from being beaten and robbed."

"That old man that you saw was my teacher. He is the one who taught me the most great name of Allah," the old man said softly.

We, as humans, have unimaginable power. We also have a great wisdom that exists deep inside that allows us to consciously use only the level of power we have developed enough wisdom to use. It is not hard to find the guidance to use the power that is our birthright. Fortunately, when we mistake our own egos for greater guidance, our inner wisdom overrules us. Like with the young man when he wanted to save the old man, he was not ready to know the most great name of Allah. He would have obviously interfered with things that he couldn't understand if he had the power. It is unlikely that any of us will ever develop the degree of wisdom needed to fully understand the complexities of life, however, we can easily develop the skills to find a greater guidance inside. We can choose to follow this guidance to the healing that is right for each of us.

You have the natural ability to heal on a deep level when you are totally in the present with any life challenge, when you dispense with the limitations of judgment or disbelief, when you have the clear intent to heal. Use this ability of being in the present to aid other means of healing whether you are using traditional or alternative medicine.

Our individual consciousness exists as a part of a ceaseless flow of universal energy—the ground of all being. Our consciousness affects our physical bodies. It is like affecting the flow of a river by placing rocks in the stream. These rocks are our thoughts. They represent our true intent. Brain researchers estimate a person thinks some 60,000 thoughts a day. This is like putting 60,000 rocks a day into our river to make it flow in the way we choose. Ninety-five percent of these thoughts are the same as we had yesterday. We use a lot of energy day after day picking up these rocks and returning them to the same place.

Thoughts are like the directors in the creation of the molecules of your body. Think back to a few years ago. The body you have now is similar to the one you had then. Of course, changes in weight, accident, illness or cosmetic surgery don't count. Your body replaces many of its cells every year; you get an entirely new one every few years. The body you had a few years ago no longer exists. Although most of your body has been replaced within this time, you probably have made few changes. Your body recreates itself using most of the same thoughts, beliefs, attitudes and emotions.

Moods and emotions have a direct effect on your body. Witness when you feel blue or down—how that affected your stance, posture and movement. Someone who has been beaten down by life has a body that reflects his dismal outlook.

Being in the present with a clear intent to heal clears the rocks in your stream of consciousness which contribute to the creation and maintenance of disease and emotional problems. These problems will be referred to in the book as *life challenges* (see pages 4-5). The following chapters will help you discover and therefore change some of the beliefs, emotions and energy that feed and maintain your life challenge. You will discover your inner guidance and learn how to follow it.

Our thoughts reflect our true intent in life. These thoughts flavor the expression of the DNA molecules as you create new cells. Newly emerging body cells are similar until they adopt the role of a specific type of cell. At the time they choose a job, so to speak, they may take on any of the billions of different functions from brain tissue to fingernails. There are even cells, called todopotential cells, that wander through your body and become any type of needed cell.

The cells of your body, as they create themselves according to DNA outlines, include the history of all life. DNA is like the storehouse of experiences of life. Within your DNA or genetic code are the elements which identify how you'll react to situations (do your run—do you fight?). This genetic coding process has not only existed in humans since their primitive beginnings, but it gives the potential which exists within the collective experience of all life.

All life is built on the foundation of previous life as witnessed in the stages of the human fetus. The first phase of development shows the fetus looking similar to a tadpole. As development continues, it goes through stages similar to that of a dog, then ape, and finally human..

Another interesting aspect of evolution, reflected in the evolutionary process of DNA, is called the "hundredth monkey principle." If you teach a monkey or any life form to do something new, the rest of its species will have an easier time learning the new task. With humans every record that is set becomes a common event in time. It's as if in some way the DNA of the same species communicates the new task, even when located on the other side of the earth. When a person does something never accomplished before, somehow the potential to do the same feat becomes available to others. Perhaps this communication takes place within the DNA or its mirror image, the RNA.

Introduction

Our immune systems are greater than any model yet suggested, though in the past Western medicine embraced the human immune system with a very limited view. Doctors emphasized the chemical balance workings of the immune system almost to the exclusion of other medical approaches. They manipulated the electrochemical dynamics (medicines) as the most common treatment of immune-related problems. In extreme cases body parts were removed, restructured or destroyed by surgery, chemotherapy or radiation therapy.

Besides certain proven modern treatments, medical professionals are now investigating subtle and noninvasive means to boost the human immune system. Different immune functions have been explored throughout history but are now being rediscovered. The French physician, A. A. Tomatis, used the chanting of Gregorian monks to prove that sound stimulates and strengthens the immune system. Dr. Tomatis suggests that immune systems improve when they are fed and charged with nourishing sound. The damaging effects of loud or noxious sound are well-known.

Osteopaths, nurses, massage therapists and chiropractors use touch and movement to stimulate neural, blood and endocrine flow. The works of Dolores Krieger, Ph.D., Brugh Joy, M.D., and Barbara Brennan, M.S., show the immune system is affected by what Brennan calls the human energy field. Robert O. Becker, M.D., has measured this energy field in his research. These and other therapeutic touch pioneers suggest the intent of the healing practitioner, patient, family and friends directly affects the energetic

aspects of immune function. Ancient energy healing practices such as qigong and acupuncture support this view.

The works of O. Carl Simonton, M.D., and Bernie
Siegel, M.D., show that belief, emotion and intent directly
affect the immune system. They found that you can explore
and alter your intent toward healing by using your imagination. Candace Pert, Ph.D., and her associates demonstrated
the role of neuropeptides in communicating emotion,
belief, and intent.

The use of light in healing also is an ancient practice.
In recent times, major research by Russian scientists involved the use of bioplasma (living energy or life energy)
and biophotons (light emitted from each body cell).

I am suggesting these, and possibly other aspects yet to
be discovered, directly affect your immune system. In this
book we will explore and experience ways to boost your
immune system which are not commonly used today in
western medicine. The exercises in this book are *not* intended to replace traditional western medical treatment.
The western physicians are highly trained professionals.
They have an understanding of the specific dynamics of
physiology and treatments that are beyond those of us
without such training. This work supplements both traditional medicine and alternative treatments.

As a reader, I want you to take responsibility for your
healing process and use the proper healing (traditional and
alternative) medical resources. I hope readers will use this
material to increase their options when facing either major
or minor life challenges. I don't want to limit making use
of the vast professional resources available; I want to foster
greater cooperation with physicians and other healing
professionals. The cooperative climate among those in the
healing arts is changing. For example, a modern pain center
today may include a neurologist, internist, anesthesiologist,

surgeon, psychiatrist, psychotherapist, hypnotherapist, spiritual therapist, osteopath, nurse, chiropractor, yoga instructor, biofeedback and relaxation therapist, massage and movement therapist, art therapist, music therapist, physical therapist, social worker and nutritionist.

One of my clients, who grew up on a farm, told me a story about his father bringing home baby chickens in the spring. They also kept eggs in incubators, and, he liked to watch them hatch. The eggs started to crack and the struggle of birth began. He told me about watching a newly hatched chick, still weak and dazed from fighting his way out of his egg. The chick staggered over to another egg just as it began to hatch, as if to say, "I'll help you. I can't stand to watch you struggle." The chick then pecked away a small piece of the shell. The struggling ceased almost immediately. Deprived of the struggle of birth, the unhatched chick died. Hatching, for a chicken, provides the movement necessary to activate the systems in its body which are necessary for continued life.

Perhaps your life challenges are the real source of your ability to live and become stronger. Nietzsche said, "That which does not kill you makes you stronger." Psychiatrist Milton Erickson often told his patients that he didn't want them to heal too soon. He taught them that within the problem is an accurate guide to the solution. And, if the person approached the problem as a friend instead of an enemy, he might find the resources to solve the problem permanently.

I want readers to learn they have an inner guidance they can use. This inner guidance or what I call *The Spunky Factor* is the creative energy to aid in self-healing. The act of seeking guidance carries an innate intent. It isn't important anyone know how this works. That isn't the purpose of this book. I believe *how* this works is unknowable.

It is easy to see how your relationship with the stresses in your world affect healing and growth. Your relationship with stress affects your body like stress affects your car. If you drive your car with anger, you drastically increase energy in the form of fuel used to get to your destination. Driving while angry causes more wear and tear and increases the odds of being in an accident. Prolonged anger does damage to your body and makes you more accident prone. If you go through life fueled by anger, fear, guilt, hatred, etc., you drain your life energy and cause excess wear on your body. These emotions are the most common and powerful motivating forces in our society. Unfortunately, these also are the most common attitudes toward healing.

A life fueled by loving respect does not create within itself the negative wear and tear. As you travel through this book, choose to fuel your journey with self-respect and compassion for yourself.

I urge you to use the training and expertise of the health care professionals to identify the appropriateness or inappropriateness of any given treatment for your unique life challenge. The intent of this writing is self-empowerment, self-respect and self-responsibility, which have a direct effect on your immune system. Like living, no one else can do it for you.

Chapter 1

Healing On the Edge of Now

Several years ago on a steamy, summer afternoon, we pulled up to a four-way stop on a country highway. I paused on my motorcycle and took time to notice the beauty of the surrounding countryside. As I started toward the intersection to make a left turn, I caught a glimpse of another motorcycle—tires screaming and brakes locked—coming right at me. An instant later its handlebars slammed into my lower back, the motorcycle flipped over my left hip and tumbled end over end into the ditch. By some miracle, I was left standing in the middle of the intersection. My heavy motorcycle fell over and pinned my rider beneath it. Without hesitating, I lifted the motorcycle off of him with one hand (a personal example of the power of our life energy). We waited a good hour before help arrived. After the police and ambulance left, I managed to steer my bent and battered bike safely home.

On the next day, I suddenly felt an extreme pain in my lower back. I knew I needed help. However, I grew up in a family where we went to see doctors only when we needed vaccinations, when something oozed from the body or when someone had a high fever. As a result, I didn't trust doctors. After ten days, my wife finally persuaded me to see a chiropractor. I trusted chiropractors even less than medical doctors. Still, I reasoned that they deal with the spine and I desperately needed help. Besides, the pain was getting too much to bear.

I found an exceptional chiropractor, named Brent. He had me fill out many forms. One form had a long checklist of about one hundred and fifty symptoms. Brent looked at me as if to say, "I've got another hypochondriac to deal with here." However, after taking a series of X-rays, he said that he was amazed I could walk into his office, and he told me the grim news. He didn't see how I could walk even before the accident. The X-rays showed fused vertebrae. We came to the conclusion that my vertebrae had probably fused because of an automobile accident I'd had at age four. Now, because of the recent motorcycle injury, Brent said that if I received a hard slap on my back or a slight rear end car collision, I would likely become paralyzed.

He said, "If your body was a house, I wouldn't step inside. A strong gust of wind might collapse it."

I asked him how I should go about healing the wounds. Brent said it was impossible. He tried, tactfully, to tell me that within ten years life in a wheelchair was almost a certainty.

I asked, "Okay, but if it was possible, how could I go about repairing the damage?"

To appease me, he showed me the X-rays again. He pointed to the most serious injury which could later sever my spinal cord. He reminded me of his findings which showed two vertebrae fused from the childhood injury. These two fused vertebrae are where I chose to start.

I asked, "How can I clean these vertebrae of calcium allowing them to move again?"

"Surgery is the only way."

"I'm only interested in how a human body might do it if a human body could." He answered with the guess that somehow the calcium would be carried off and eliminated one grain at a time.

As I mentioned before, I seldom went to doctors. However, while growing up I did learn countless examples from my mother of the power of focused imaging. She had learned these techniques from my grandmother, who had learned them from my full-blooded Cherokee Indian great-grandmother. Throughout my life I had found the powers of the mind to be available and very potent. As a result, I began to picture tiny beings inside my body whose job was to handle the transfer of calcium to be used or discarded. I called these beings *terriers* and talked to them every day. I told them how they had been lazy or forgetful and had been leaving this calcium lying around where it hindered my back.

In my thoughts, I often heard the song, *Working in the Coal Mine*. In every spare moment, I imagined the terriers at work diligently removing the calcium. I checked in (scanned my spine) several times a day to keep track of their progress. With my mind's eye, I saw the mass of calcium growing smaller. This translated to the "real" world with the fact that my vertebrae slowly were beginning to move again. After eighteen months the calcium had dissolved to a thumbnail-shaped sliver and I suddenly felt a piercing pain. It felt like my upper vertebrae were grinding against the lower vertebrae.

I accepted the pain as a sign of definite progress. Although, after a couple months of being in constant companionship with the pain, I had myself convinced that it could be a tumor. I returned to my chiropractor for new X-rays. Brent was on vacation and at my insistence his replacement took X-rays. After retaking the X-rays several times, he gave me the bad news. He showed me the sliver of calcium digging into my vertebrae and suggested I find a neurosurgeon—fast. I was delighted. He couldn't understand my joy. The X-rays confirmed what my inner senses told me. I was indeed doing the impossible. My inner terriers were sent back to work with renewed vigor. After a couple of months, the pain disappeared completely.

About a year-and-a-half after the accident I jokingly asked Brent, "Is it all right for me to go skydiving now?"

"Only idiots jump out of airplanes!"

He told me that sky-diving presents a danger for permanent back and ankle injury for anyone. He finished with telling me, "There is no medical reason that you shouldn't sky-dive—if that's what you want to do."

I was shocked. "I thought you told me I'd wind up in a wheelchair right after my first landing."

He said that he would never have believed it possible, but I had healed well enough in his opinion that he felt I could do anything I chose to do. What impressed me was that my back had healed in spite of the chiropractor's diagnosis, even though his forecast wasn't something that I ever believed in from the start. What amazed me most— my twenty-year old injuries also had healed!

I was able to heal as a result of the combination of Brent's healing skills and my willingness to do the required work daily. My healing surprised him. He couldn't understand why I had healed from this type of injury. Through hindsight, I realize that the calcium that fused the vertebrae together acted as a natural cast which allowed my childhood injury to heal.

What exactly is a *life challenge*? Throughout your life there are barriers to fulfillment. There are barriers to having what you want and being happy. Barriers sometimes exist against having satisfying and nurturing relationships. During your life you will encounter barriers that limit the quality of life in some way; I call these barriers, life challenges.

Most life challenges result from beliefs and of emotional charges that we attach to different areas of our lives. Some challenges may be physical, such as cancer or multiple sclerosis, but most are less concrete, less life threatening. Other life challenges are emotional charges: anger, hate, jealousy, greed and so on. Even subtle life challenges related to forgotten hurts and fears make up a part of living.

It's not hard to see how our relationships with life affect our health. If you live stressfully most of the time, your constant overreaction may lead to stroke, ulcers, cancer or heart attack.

In short, a life challenge is anything that interferes with living in a deeply satisfying and fulfilling way. Only you can know what brings satisfaction and fulfillment. Often, even to know what brings satisfaction and fulfillment is a confusing issue for people. Most creatures on this earth aren't confused about what it takes to be successful and fulfilled. Look at an animal's life. If a deer survives, has enough to eat, runs free and raises its young, the deer is a success in life. With people it's different. No one knows what is satisfying or fulfilling for you. You must decide.

My current back injury provided the opportunity to heal the earlier emotional and physical life challenge of the fused vertebrae. Surgery and a body cast became unnecessary; my body removed the fused calcium. As my spine healed, I worked through some childhood traumas and released many old beliefs, emotions and attitudes. My lifestyle changed—so did the way I treated myself and others. The quality of my relationships was changing as well. Ignoring my doctor's beliefs, I chose to heal myself. I used the tools that were natural and easily available to me (music, imagery and the willingness to change).

The changes touched every area of my life. They happened without my being aware of their scope. I now worked with what my mind, body and spirit presented to me. I followed the guidance that occurred naturally by the process of working toward an active and healthier life. The changes that grew out of this movement toward healing created a robust, stronger Carl.

A series of exercises to develop inner guidance are included throughout the book. It's very important you do each exercise in sequence to build a base for firsthand experience of your inner resources. The purpose of the exercises is to acquaint you with how your health is affected by your relationships with your inner and outer worlds. Each exercise is designed so you can see and learn ways to control your immune function. Like riding a bicycle, the real learning is in the experience. You can talk about it until you understand every detail of how to do it. Yet, until you get on the bike, fall and get up several times, you really won't know and feel the experience of controlling the bicycle. With these exercises, you won't skin your knee. They are only meant to increase your awareness of your inner and outer world. You experience what you experience, and that is all that's important. You may do these exercises anytime or anyplace.

There should not be any undue effort or struggle to learn these exercises. Don't force anything. Being tense and desperate are obstacles to your healing process. The only strife in healing is what we project on it with our beliefs and emotions. Learning to relax and let go are your friends.

The exercises should be read very slowly and leisurely, using a pleasant voice. Time needs to be given for each image form. Your voice needs to convey that there is nothing else in the world that is important right now except to experience in the here and now. If your mind wanders while you read these, it will be reflected in your voice.

I suggest that you record these exercises for your own repeated use. Some people prefer to hear their own voice guiding them, others prefer another voice to their own.

Grounding

The first step in any subtle energy work, like boundary perception, is to increase your presence. Presence is simply being here with no thoughts of the past or future, just attending to now with all your senses. Complete presence is a feat seldom achieved.

The Buddhists know the value of presence. They go through extensive training in the art of being present. The tea ceremony is an exercise in presence. During the ceremony, everyone is expected to be completely focused on the events and yet have no thoughts about it.

The easiest, quickest and most readily learned method of increasing presence is grounding. Grounding allows you to become more aware of your body. Emotional content often emerges in the form of various bodily sensations as you develop presence. The pain you feel in your body may be emotional in origin as often as it is physical. If you bring your awareness to the pain, the emotional aspects may become apparent to you. The following brief exercise begins to bring awareness into your body in a nonthreatening way.

There are many kinds of grounding exercises. This one is done in the style of Life Energy Fundamentals®, developed by Pamela and Jeff Krock. Their Training in Life Energy Fundamentals® teaches people to consciously be

Life Energy Fundamentals® is a trademark of Pamela and Jeff Krock.

aware of, and direct, their life energy. "The fundamentals" are the fundamental ways we relate to our world energetically or with our soft bodies (thus the name)

As you go through the following grounding exercise notice how your sensual acuity changes as you become more grounded. Notice how grounding affects your feeling of safety and well-being. Notice how it affects your sense of time.

To begin this exercise, I invite you to sit upright with your feet flat on the floor. Take three deep breaths and begin to settle in your body and begin to notice where you are right now. How much of your body are you aware of? Just notice without the need to do anything, without judgment. Just notice where you are at. I, now, invite you to begin to bring your awareness to the bottoms of your feet. How aware of your feet are you right now? Just begin to bring more awareness into your feet. Bring more awareness to the soles of your feet. Let every cell become alive and aware all the way from the tips of your toes to your heels . . . the pads of your toes. Now feel the curls of your toes and the balls of your feet . . . your arches . . . feel the heels, the outside edges of your feet . . . your entire foot at once. I'd like to invite you to notice now that with the bottoms of your feet you can feel whatever they are resting on. If you are wearing socks, I invite you to notice that you can feel the material of the socks . . . you can feel the weave of the socks. You can let that feeling go a little deeper.

If you're wearing shoes, you can feel the soles of your shoes. You can feel the way they're made and the materials that they're made of. And you can let that feeling move a little deeper going out a little farther . . . you can feel the floor, perhaps it's carpeted. Perhaps it's wood or tile. Whatever it is, just notice that it feels different from the soles of your shoes and your socks. Let your awareness reach into it like roots, going deeper . . . spreading out farther. And let that feeling move down to whatever is beneath the top layer of the floor.

Perhaps that is wood or concrete. Just notice that it feels different. It feels more stable, more secure. Let those roots go deeper, now, right through the building you're in, perhaps moving through many floors, or through a basement. Just let the roots keep going until they reach into the earth. Notice that you can feel the texture of the earth beneath the building. You can feel the coolness . . . the darkness. You can feel the moisture content. Let the roots go as deep as you choose now, even all the way through the earth if that feels right.

Roots have two purposes; one is for strength and stability and the other is to bring back nourishment and information. So I invite you now to just experience the way things are different now as you do the grounding. Notice the quality of your senses and your degree of serenity. Just take as much time as you choose to delight yourself as you explore this realm of grounding. Take all the time you choose and when you're ready, just allow your eyes to open and your consciousness to return to the room around you.

This grounding exercise is from Tai Chi martial arts and reveals some benefits of grounding. This exercise requires two people. Person #1 stands relaxed with a normal state of mind. Person #2 gently pushes #1's shoulder until he is pushed off balance. The first person now imagines roots growing deep into the earth from his feet and the second person again pushes. Both partners now feel that person #1 is more solid and harder to push off balance. Repeat the sequence only this time, person #1 brings his awareness to his pelvis and the roots from his feet. His stability again increases. Repeat several times and then switch roles with your partner.

Soft Body

This exercise introduces you to the soft body concept and helps increase awareness of what is going on inside.

I invite you now to return to the state of grounding. Noticing that each time you do the grounding exercise you become more aware of things—that you become more solid, more stable in the world. So, just let the roots become deeper and denser now—just let them spread out. There's an aspect of existence that when it is absent, our bodies become corpses. There are many names for this aspect. In this exercise we will call it the soft body. I'd like to invite you now to bring your awareness back to your feet and while you extend your roots deep into the earth, just notice how much of your feet you're aware of. Are your toes full of awareness? And how does the awareness fill your heels? The tops of your feet? Just notice how your consciousness fits in your feet. Do you fill your feet fully from heel to toe? From side to side? And top to bottom? And is this awareness or your soft body centered in your bones? How does it fit into your ankles? Is it aligned and centered there? Is there any twisting or moving from one side or another? Is there any rising up? Just notice without judgment or the need to do anything about it.

And how is your awareness filling your lower legs at this moment? If your legs were vases and the awareness, the consciousness, or the soft body was water, how would that water be filling your legs right now? Are there places that resist filling? Places where the awareness concentrates? Is your awareness centered in your bones. Is there any twisting . . . moving forward or backward or to either side? Are you long enough there? And how do you align from your knees to your hips? Are you centered and aligned in your bones? Are your upper legs full of awareness all the way to the skin? Does it move forward or backward? Is it too long or too short? Just notice. Now, I wonder how you align with your hips. Are they squared and centered? And is your pelvis full of awareness? Or are there places that don't seem to be aware, or places that are numb? Maybe there are places where the awareness is really concentrated, perhaps almost burning . . . just notice.

And notice how you're aligned with your spine now. Do you have the full length of your spine? Are you centered with it? Is there any twisting . . . pushing forward or backward . . . zigzagging back and forth? And notice your torso. How do you infuse your torso with awareness? Are you aware of the inner workings of your inner organs? Are you aware of your heart beating . . . of the air moving in and out of your lungs, passing through your mouth and nose? Just notice how you fill your torso . . . where the awareness might find resistance. Where it might be concentrated. Notice your fingers now.

How do you align with the bones of your fingers and hands? Are you centered in the bones of your fingers, hands and wrists. How do you align with your lower arms? Just notice. From wrist to elbow to shoulder, how does your soft body awareness infuse your arms and shoulders?

And how does it fill your head? Do you infuse your entire brain with energy or awareness or only specific parts . . . just notice. And how alive are the senses that are centered in your head? Sight, sound, taste, smell, touch and the inner equivalents; the inner eye, the inner ear, the other senses . . . just notice. Take as much time as you choose to experience your soft body and how it infuses your physical body.

When you're ready, just let your eyes open naturally and easily and allow your consciousness to return to the room around you.

Mindfulness

Grounding helps establish a state of mind known as mindfulness. Mindfulness is necessary for all subtle energy work of this nature. Mindfulness is a state of being aware with all your senses. You observe in an impersonal way without judgment or the need to take any action. See through the eyes of the one inside who sees through your eyes. Listen to the one who listens inside. It is the *silent reporter* position. A good reporter reports the observable facts without interjecting his own judgment.

Wu Wei

Another useful attitude when doing these exercises is wu wei. Wu wei (pronounced *woo-way*) is a Chinese term for moving through life with ease. Wu wei is the art of being present with each moment of your life without the constant chatter of the inner voices. The practices of Zen, Yoga, Taoism and martial arts all use exercises for developing inner silence and presence. When practicing wu wei, you meet each moment of life with an attitude of nonjudgment and a demeanor of inner silence.

If your house falls down, you simply begin to rebuild it without the constant overreaction that drains your energy and harms your health. In any situation, no matter how drastic, you take what in essence is the right direction. This doesn't mean you deny your feelings. It means you feel more fully, having no judgements about yourself or what you are feeling. It is acceptance and release as a manner of walking the earth with practical feet and getting on with your life.

To be most effective, you must approach your own

healing with wu wei. It's a soft focus to being here and now. Paul Reps summed it up in two words, "Be, lightly."

The key attitudes emphasized throughout the rest of the book are *mindfulness, being grounded, and being centered.*

Chapter 2

Approaches to Psychoneuroimmunology

Psychoneuroimmunology (PNI) is the study and practice of sharing in our own healing. *Psycho* deals with the mind, or our ability to choose, or to have intent. *Neuro* deals with the brain and nervous system. *Immunology* deals with the body's natural immune defenses such as white blood cells, T-cells and macrophages. PNI also is the study of how and why we can directly influence our healing with our beliefs and emotions.

The practice of PNI, while it has only recently received the acceptance of the American Medical Association, is not new. Many ancient cultures and religions used some form of PNI. The Taoist priests of China collected more than sixteen hundred volumes on an energy transformative form of healing called Qigong.

The modern study of PNI started in the late 1950's. An amazing boy in a hospital in Massachusetts shocked the world's medical community. He had an inoperable grapefruit-sized brain tumor that was growing larger every day. His family felt each trip to the hospital might be his last.

Following some inner guidance, the boy intuitively began to play a video game of pretend in his mind. Perhaps angels guided him. No one will ever know why he began to imagine that white space ships were flying around in his brain, blasting space rays (laser beams of light) at his tumor. In the following weeks he not only imagined the tumor away, but baffled the medical world by his remarkable recovery. As the tumor shrunk in his imagination, so did the tumor in his brain.

During the early stages of research, the practice of PNI was crude. Except for a few brilliant healing professionals, such as Milton Erickson, M.D., psychoneuroimmunology (PNI) involved patients imagining white blood cells in some symbolic form. They imagined space ships, white knights or white dogs attacking and killing the invading forces of the disease. At first, the little boy's space ship format was followed by others since it was the only well-documented case of spontaneous remission available to investigators. Researchers soon added hypnosis, guided imagery and meditation to PNI. The heightened sensitivity caused by these altered states of awareness began to shed light on the emotional and energetic aspects of the human immune system.

Researchers discovered that the white blood cells and all other body cells have receptor sites for the same neurotransmitters that signal emotion in the brain. Candace Pert's neuropeptide studies have proven that the cells in your immune system feel the same emotions as you feel. So, if you are depressed every aspect of your being, including your immune system, becomes depressed.

In absence of other medical options, using *belief* as a placebo to aid healing, is an honored tradition in the medical community. A placebo is a kind of trick used by doctors. The medication has no known medical effects, yet, in certain cases the patient recovers. Placebos have often provided remarkable healings since the beginning of recorded history. Most doctors use them successfully many times throughout their careers.

Today, PNI involves the study of systemic disease by way of two opposing medical approaches. The allopathic or traditional approach is mainly concerned with your body's electrochemical properties. Doctors change specific balances with drugs and medical technology to help restore you to health. For instance, antibiotics fight bacterial infections by wiping out most of the infectious bacteria. Killing the harmful bacteria gives the helpful bacteria a chance to reestablish itself. This is like poisoning a lake to kill most of the sucker fish so the trout can survive. It's like shaking one side of a mobile to untangle the strings on the opposite side.

The homeopathic approach helps restore you to health by strengthening weak body systems through stimulating them directly. If you go to a homeopath with a bacterial infection, he might give you something to increase the helpful bacteria. The good bacteria subdues the infectious bacteria and brings the patient back to a healthful condition.

This is similar to adding weight to an undersized figure on a mobile in order to create balance. If your liver function is poor, a doctor of homeopathy might give you a potion that supplies the frequency of energetic vibration which is needed to bring the liver back to normal. It's as if the vibration of the potion resonates with something in the liver and causes a vibratory reaction. When you strike a tuning fork and bring it close to another tuning fork of the same frequency, the unstruck tuning fork starts to vibrate and produce sound.

One way of looking at disease is that it is an invading force to be conquered. Another way is to approach disease as a difficult relationship that may be transformed into a healthy relationship. Each approach has its proper place.

For example, a diabetic may prevent the damaging effects of the disease through diet and exercise. In this way, he transforms the relationship from a life threatening challenge to an opportunity for promoting a healthful lifestyle. This is a process of self-realization and adjustment of beliefs, attitudes and emotions. If you ignore diet and exercise, then a ripe environment for the disease may occur.

In PNI, we may shake a belief system to untangle limiting beliefs. Or, we may work directly with emotion or body energy to change an unhealthy balance.

The Soft Body

I adopted the name, *soft body*, to label the energetic aspect of all living things. It's also known as the light body, the energy body, the soul, the holy ghost, ki, chi and shakti. Whatever you call it, an invisible force inhabits our bodies. When it is gone, our bodies become corpses. However, while you are alive in your body, you can learn to control this energy.

The soft body does whatever we direct it to do. The soft body, like our material physical body, has capabilities we can't understand. Just because we have no idea how our muscles, joints, bones, and chemicals work, doesn't mean we can't walk. We walk because we have, under our memory control, the means to walk. And more important, we believe we can walk and we keep trying until we learn. We also have this less solid body that we use constantly even though we pretend it doesn't exist. The pretending that the soft body doesn't exist is the training of our society— the physical or material realm is all that exists and is the only thing that matters.

Researchers, under the direction of Robert O. Becker,

M.D., have measured the soft body under laboratory conditions. They found a constant low voltage direct current (DC) field that infuses the body with life. There are perineural cells at the end of every nerve that act as a transceiver for this DC energy field. It is theorized these cells are the energetic frameworks that act as a mold in which the body forms. They induced anesthesia in salamanders by reversing the polarity of this energy flow in the brain. On the other hand, they overrode chemically-induced anesthesia by increasing the flow of energy in a drugged salamander's brain. They proved that in healing, the higher the energy or consciousness in the injured area, the quicker the healing took place. In work with tumors, they found that a tumor would continue growing despite the polarity of the direct current.

Directing and aiding healing is a function of the soft body. Although it takes practice to learn, you don't have to strain. The soft body responds perfectly to our intent in life. As you use this energy in your healing, you learn to use these abilities everyday with truth, compassion and respect. Words are necessary to motivate you to learn to use your soft body, but experience puts you in touch with the real, healing energy. This is where pure unclouded guidance is to be discovered.

Symbols, such as words or visual images describe the relationships your soft body has with your physical world—and the relationships it has with the total pool of consciousness. It is easy to access this essential guidance or consciousness, but without adequate symbols to express the existence of this consciousness we seem to lack the faith needed to follow this guidance.

The study of physics tells us that all things are created from a universal energy. This universal energy is the essential building block of all things. Evolutionary theory says that consciousness began to express itself as life. The first organisms on earth were simple life forms. Each life form possesses more potential for experiencing the world as it becomes more complex. Cats are able to experience more than amoebas, but less than humans. It might seem that the only purpose of this universal energy or consciousness is to express itself in a way that provides experience. Perhaps, Stephen Levine is right in stating that the only nourishment of the soul is experience.

Water, as it moves ceaselessly, never separating, is a good metaphor for the way universal energy infuses everything. Your body is almost entirely water. A certain amount of water moves through your body everyday and must be replaced. You may be drinking water that was once consumed by a desert camel or by another human such as Sitting Bull. As water passes through your system, you flavor it with wastes that are excreted in the form of vapor from your breath, sweat, urine and feces. The water in all these wastes is connected to the vapor in the air, the water in and around the earth, and the water in your body. The water in your body, like the air you breath, is not something that you ever really own. Both are only yours to share as they pass through your body. Air and water are both like living bodies that are in constant change.

We share the life of these bodies with all things on earth, living and non-living. If it is true that all things are made entirely of essential energy and this essential energy is pure consciousness, then the water and the air in your body has the potential to be aware of all water and all air everywhere through it's connection with the universal water body and air body. In their ceaseless movement water and air touch and pass through all things. This provides a universal connection with all things that contain water and air. On a soft body level this same dynamic can be experienced.

Where Is the Center of Your Universe?

Sit erect with your feet on the floor and take a deep breath. Settle into your body and become more grounded. With your eyes closed, bring your awareness to one inch in front of your spine. Notice where this awareness seems to be in relation to your physical spine. The location of this awareness changes from moment to moment. Sometimes it is even outside your physical body. Now, make a mental picture of the world around you. Notice if more of your world is in front of you or behind you. Notice if you sense more world existing to your left or to your right.

Notice if more of your world is above you or below you. Do you exist at the center of your world (or reality) or have you placed yourself off center? Are you to the front, back, either side, above or below or a combination of any of the above? Notice if you exist more inside or outside your body. Which is larger, inside or outside? During the day, notice where you place yourself in your world.

Water Exercise

I'd like to invite you now to just begin to settle into your body. Begin to adjust yourself into a very comfortable position. I'm going to tell you a story. You don't need to even listen to this story, you can just attend to the delightful things you might discover in your body. The things you may have overlooked before. This is a story about you. About a very small part of a greater part of who you really are. You know this story well. So, there's no need to listen. There's a part of you that will take care of that.

A while back I went to the mountains. I lay down by a mountain stream where it ran through a beautiful mountain meadow. It was a warm sunny day. As I lay there looking up at the sky, it brought me back to childhood and the times, on a spring or summer or fall day, when I'd lay on the grass and look up at the sky, smelling the freshly watered lawn. Feeling the blades of grass as they embraced my body, tickling little bitty parts of my skin. I'd lay there and just let gravity support and embrace me as I watched the sky. Sometimes there would be clouds. Sometimes there would be big fluffy clouds floating against a clear blue sky. Sometimes there were little dark clouds racing against a background of gray wispy clouds. And sometimes it seemed as if the clouds went on forever.

I lay there next to the mountain stream, listening to the sound of the water, listening to the water as it rippled over rocks and letting that sound move right through my body. It's as if it vibrated inside of me as the sound of the water coursed through my body. The mountain sun warm on my skin. The smell of the water and pine trees rich in the air. Birds singing and playing. And in my imagination, as if I were a child still watching the sky, I climbed into a boat in the stream. And as I lay there on the bank, I could feel the boat rising and falling beneath me, being jostled back and forth and from side to side in the stream's current. Up and down as I began to float down stream. And as I continued past the rocks and the trees, past the deer, deep into the forest and suddenly I plunged into the forest where all other sound disappears—as if absorbed by the sound of the wind blowing in the tops of the trees, sounding very much like the ocean. I heard the constant roar of the wind.

Then suddenly the stream and the boat I was in plunged into the earth, taking me deep underground. The sound of the earth grew louder as I plunged deeper and deeper. I felt so safe and comfortable as if being in the womb of the earth. And as I followed the water through the veins of the earth,

I could sense that water permeated every part of the earth's body. And suddenly, the stream emerged and there was a cave. The cave looked out over the mountain valley below and the water fell crashing to the rocks below with the sound thundering inside. Thundering in my brain, thundering in my body, thundering in my mind. Thundering in my heart, with the realization that the water in the earth is like the blood in my body. The blood in my body is made mainly of water. My entire body is mainly water. And then I began to wonder, what happens to the water that leaves my body?

So, I put a special vibration, a special color and a special scent on the moisture in my breath so I could follow it anywhere. I followed this vapor as it rose in the sky joining with the moisture in the clouds. The clouds became heavy with water and it began to fall to the earth, right through the rising mist. Some of the rain even evaporated on the way down and began to rise back up to the clouds. The water moving both ways at once, moving through itself in opposite directions. Some of the raindrops hit the earth and began to soak into the ground. Some formed little rivulets that joined with the spider web-like formation of water that goes through the earth from one side to the other, joining it all at once. All the way through the earth and into the atmosphere.

I followed that water. Some of it formed rivers and lakes and eventually fed the oceans. And some of it flowed back into that little mountain stream that I lay next to listening to the gurgling water. And I realized that all living things on this earth share this living body of water. It constantly flows through all of us at once. All connected from the solid state of ice, the liquid state of water, the gaseous state of steam. All connected. No separation.

I'd like to invite you now to take all the time you choose to savour the experiences of the journey you have just been on. I invite you to choose to be open to the new possibilities that you may see with your mind's eye, that you may hear with your inner ear, that you may know and feel in your heart and belly. Take all the time you choose. When you're ready, just let your eyes open and your consciousness return to the room around you.

Your soft body is like the water and air that your physical body contains in that it has the illusion of being separate from the total pool of essential energy, yet, it is not separate. It is not possible to separate yourself from the universal energy. Your body provides the means to experience not only your personal life energy but any part of the universal energy as well.

The Eagle

You will find The Eagle to be a special energizing and uplifting exercise.

I invite you to begin to ground yourself and settle into your body. Begin to become centered. Just notice what's going on inside right now. Just begin to follow your breath inward. Breathing deeper and deeper with each breath. Your breath moving deeper into your body and farther back with each breath. And I invite you now to imagine a tap root beginning at the base of your skull, following your spine downward, out your tail bone and deep into the earth . . . reaching all the way to the molten center of the earth. Through this tap root now you can begin to release anything that is appropriate to let go of at this time and send it to the earth's core to be vaporized by the intense heat. You might choose to release attitudes or beliefs that don't serve you, the so called negative attitudes and beliefs. You might choose to release toxicity of any sort, emotional, physical, spiritual or what ever it may be. Just release it into the core of the earth . . . pushing it downward with each breath.

Imagine now, that at the very tip of this tap root at the core of the earth is a vibration, like the buzzing of a bumble bee flapping it's wings. I invite you to notice that you can feel that same buzzing and flapping at the end of your tail bone. Just allow that vibration to begin to expand like a hummingbird flapping it's wings at your tail bone. And let it amplify even more as if it were a larger bird. The wings of this bird begin to tickle the insides of your hips as it flaps and it begins to rise, slowly moving up toward your chest, massaging all that it touches with awareness, bringing it to life. It flies right out through the center of your chest and then suddenly, way off in the distance you see an eagle. A huge magnificent eagle, floating on the air currents, floating high above the ground. The feathers rippling in the wind actually roaring from the sound of the wind moving through its feathers. Able to see a blade of grass a mile below and see and feel the sound of the earth itself . . . the song of the mountains and oceans even though they may be thousands of mile away.

And all of a sudden you notice that each time the eagle's wings rise there is a gentle tugging at the center your chest, in your heart area. Each time they rise, you feel the strength of those magnificent wings gently and lovingly pulling at your heart. And then you notice that as the wings fall there's a release in your heart. Rise and pull, fall and release. Rise and pull, fall and release. Rise and pull, fall and release. The eagle begins to fly toward you. Now it begins to get close enough for you to make out the details of the feathers, the beak and the talons. Suddenly, it transforms into a sphere of spinning light. You notice now that the light in the sphere is the exact same color as the light in your heart.

You realize that this is part of your heart. It has always been a part of your heart. As it moves closer, you choose to open yourself to allow the sphere to return to your heart where it belongs. Let it merge now. Just experience what you experience now without any judgment. Notice what you're feeling and what you're knowing. Take all the time you need or want. When you're ready, just allow your eyes to open and your consciousness to return to the room around you.

As mentioned before, the essential life energy that infuses the human body has been isolated and measured as a field of direct current electricity. This process uses perineural cells to communicate between various parts of the body. By projecting the soft body of another inside your own physical body, you are able to know them as if they were you. In our daily lives we do this unconsciously and in many cases never discover that what we thought was ourselves was actually our connections to others, or to beliefs or things. You may have noticed that sometimes you do things that you would normally not do, but it is expected of you so you do it anyway. Think of the child that gets into trouble with no reason except that he was compelled to do something because of parent expectations. Often, you behave as others expect you to behave. Being able to maintain boundaries with others and knowing where your boundaries end and others begin is very important for your health. This confusion is a constant source of stress.

Boundaries

What are boundaries? Whether in therapy or life the use of the term boundaries is common. Still, the nature of boundaries is usually only defined in terms of the negative results of having poor boundaries. We speak of boundaries in terms of lack of boundaries, enmeshment or failure to separate ourselves from others' boundaries. We see the dynamics of poor boundaries in cases of depression or schizophrenia, but we seldom realize our own boundaries. Experiencing your energetic boundaries and your energetic relationships with other people is essential to recognizing the influence of other people on you and your health as well as your subtle influences on them. Therapists often ask their clients to develop good boundaries without giving them a working definition of what a boundary is , let alone differences between a good boundary and a poor boundary. There are simple exercises used to increase awareness of boundaries. Some are presented here.

Perceiving Body Energy

The following two-person exercises will help to develop awareness of your energetic aspects using your own senses.

Take a few moments to become grounded. Have one person lie down. Move about ten to twelve feet from this person. With your hand open and your palm pointed toward the person, slowly begin to move closer to the person. As you come closer, notice any sensations you feel in your palm. You may feel warmth or cold. You may feel a vibration or roughness. There are many sensations you may feel. Whatever you feel is right. Therapeutic touch practitioners say that there are seven layers of subtle sensations (energy layers) that you may feel as you continue to approach until you touch the other person. Notice how many layers you feel. It is unlikely that you can feel all seven layers the first time you try this.

If you are the person lying down, notice how it feels to

be approached this way. How is it different with your eyes closed? How does it feel to have someone move through the energy layers?

If possible, have a different person lie down now and notice the differences in the feel of the energy field between the two. Use several more people, if available, and note any similarities or differences among them.

A growing number of registered nurses practice therapeutic touch in hospitals. Therapeutic touch proves itself to be a wonderful aid in the treatment of various health problems. The best feature of therapeutic touch is that it's easy to learn. An adult family member can learn to take over treatment in a few hours. Using energy to aid in healing is a powerful healing technique that anyone can learn. If you find this work intriguing, ask any nurse and they may be able tell you where to get competent training.

In the practice of modern medicine, as we've said before, doctors measure human energy fields in many ways in the diagnosis of disease and injury. There are EKGs, MRIs, EEGs, CAT and PET scans. We cannot dispute these energy fields or that they reflect certain health facts about patients. We already know that people can feel and use this energy. How does this affect our daily lives? An exercise from Ron Kurtz's *Body-Centered Psychotherapy, The Hakomi Method* follows.

The Power of Touch

Do this exercise with two people. Start by grounding. One person sits in a comfortable position in a state of mindfulness. The other person waits until the first person is ready and then begins to move her hand very slowly, with palm open, toward the first person. Both people note the automatic reactions occurring within their minds and bodies as the hand approaches to touch a prearranged spot on the first person's body. I suggest you touch the person's shoulder or face. Ask where he or she wants to be touched and under no circumstances should you touch the genitals or women's breasts. The second person allows the touch, with palm open, to rest gently on the first person for about ten seconds and then very slowly moves the hand away. Both people should notice anything, no matter how subtle, which happens as the touch lingers and then as the hand is removed. Have them talk about their experiences while they are happening. Repeat the above sequence and then reverse roles. If the person being touched has any feeling of discomfort from the approaching hand, have them hold the wrist of the approaching hand. By guiding the hand, this gives them the power to stop the touch at any point. With touch, safety is of supreme importance.

Next, both partners take time to ground. Imagine connecting from heart to heart, like connecting with roots. Remember, roots have two purposes—one is for strength and stability and the other is to bring back nourishment and information. Repeat the exercise with the heart to heart connection and notice any difference.

You probably experienced some emotion during the preceding exercise. This may have been anything from a slight feeling of contentment or anxiety to catharsis or extreme fear. This exercise shows the touch that causes the most profound reaction in us isn't always the physical touch. Once we enter the boundaries of the energy field of another person, it seems that we cause a reaction in that person and in ourselves. Let's explore how far away we have to be to cause a reaction in another person with another exercise from Ron Kurtz.

Learning to experience your soft body directly, without

the need to describe your relationship with it provides you with a source of unlimited wisdom and healing power. If you notice, you will probably find that you go through life describing every detail to yourself. You may describe the most common things to yourself as if you had never seen them before. You directly experience the world; you are aware of what you experience, but you are still compelled to describe what you have experienced over and over again. Who are you narrating for? Why must you describe what you experience to yourself? Is it possible that you are stating the limits of reality that you are willing to experience?

Your descriptions are not as reliable as your direct experience. Imagine the difference between being in Hawaii and reading about being in Hawaii. The way we experience the world is like going to Hawaii, staying in a hotel room, reading about the marvels that exist outside the door, but not having the time to experience them, because we are too busy reading descriptions of them.

When Does a Touch Begin?

This exercise is to be done in pairs. Both partners should take a few minutes to get grounded and go into a state of mindfulness. One person stands against a wall with their eyes closed while the other approaches silently from a distance of at least twenty feet. I recommend a longer approach if possible. The receiving person will raise their hand each time they would like the approaching person to stop, allowing the receiver more time to feel the sensations. The approaching person then stops until the receiving person drops their arm. The approaching person continues until he is only a few inches from the receiver. The receiver then opens her eyes to check the distance between the two. The receiver closes her eyes again while the approaching person silently backs away to the original position.

Change roles and repeat the process. If there are two or more pairs, partners should change and repeat the exercise. Try different variations like one person walking toward two or three others, or two people walking simultaneously toward one person. Approach from the side or back of the first person. Notice the different ways this exercise affects you emotionally and how it affects your sense of well-being and feeling of safety. Notice the distance from which you can feel another or be felt by them and the way that your approach affects another. Sense the quality of your feelings and any other aspect that may interest you.

Repeat the preceding exercises. This time, have the approaching person choose a situation or incident that evokes strong emotion from them. Have them hold these images in their mind as they again approach. Partners, take notice of any difference in their experience.

Next, have the approached person ground. Then imagine all their life energy being drawn into an imaginary egg shell surrounding their body. Have people approach now, while experiencing strong emotion and have each person notice any difference in the experience. This is a quick and easy way to experience and learn to work with your boundaries.

You have probably experienced that your awareness extends some distance from your body. And, it overlaps others' awareness. In other words, you become enmeshed in and violate other people's boundaries as you interact with them. Grounding by itself creates a feeling of increased safety and protection. It promotes centering, thus creating more safety. Grounding and centering (as experienced in the soft body exercise) help to create and maintain distinct bodily boundaries.

The Inner Child

There are a growing number of body-oriented psychotherapies that use body sensations to reach the inner child within us. These techniques may include hands-on work, but most commonly involve focusing your awareness on the feelings that occur in your body when you recall a past event. In remembering an event, you relate to it in certain ways. You see and react to it in a way consistent with your overall beliefs.

You adopt a physical stance or posturing that also affirms your belief about the event. If you believe there is danger, your body braces to fight or run away. Your brain signals to the rest of your nervous system to speed up certain chemicals and slow others to prepare your body for action.

Body-oriented psychotherapists focus on the physical aspects of the event. If you think about an event, your body reacts in a subtle manner as if in the original event. When you focus on and amplify this reaction, the emotional and belief patterns that you originally felt become clear.

Your physical symptoms, emotions and beliefs reflect how you see and feel about yourself, the people in your life, your physical environment, and your spiritual beliefs and practices. Your symptoms are part of the physical expression of your harmony or lack of harmony with your total environment. You can interact with the physical and emotional expressions of your life challenge the way you might interact with a child—an inner child here.

The purpose is to discover the needs of the inner child and release the negative emotions or limiting beliefs that you are still playing out in your life. Often it's as if we were traumatized by something during childhood. A part of our awareness breaks off to protect us from the long forgotten event. This awareness (a child's awareness) continues to defend itself in a silent, underground way from a distant danger. The inner child doesn't realize that he or she survived the assault. Reaction from the child protecting itself becomes chronic, background tension for the adult. The trauma the child defends against may be either actual or imagined fear. Trauma also may have happened as an adult from something as common as feeling unappreciated in the family or extended family. The inner child becomes trapped in a specific part of the body. Beliefs and emotional prison bars hold it there.

Your inner child calls out for help and a physical symptom develops. The longer you ignore the child, the louder the protest becomes. This isn't to say that the inner child causes or creates the life challenge. It's more like the offspring of all the stresses in our lives. The stressors create fertile ground for the development of life challenges. We might view this stress as the parents of the inner child or pathology.

The Boundaries of Belief; The Prison of Emotion

Each person does the best they can in accordance with their beliefs.
—Barry Neil Kaufman, *Happiness Is a Choice*

Beliefs are like taking a trip and setting the limits of the scenery we will see. Our beliefs decide how we see our experiences. It's as if the scenery we pass through in our life's journey is painted on the canvas of our minds and projected around us. The mechanics of vision show how this works. When we open our eyes and see the world, what our eyes are seeing and what our mind's eye is seeing are two different things. Our physical eyes pick up images that are upside down and distorted. The images from the eyes are transmitted to the brain where they are turned rightside up and stretched out. The brain fills in the details according to the beliefs and conditioning it operates by. We choose what we overlook by what we pay attention to.

All experiences somehow fit into the boundaries of our total beliefs. We choose how we feel about what we see within these belief boundaries. Our bodies react to what is happening within our boundaries. Of course every person sees, feels and reacts in their own unique way.

We selectively tune out much of our daily world. The only way we can describe anything to ourselves is with the words and ideas we know. We overlook anything that doesn't fit our beliefs because to us it doesn't exist. If we are aware enough to notice something, we must alter it to fit into our belief system.

There is a movie entitled, *The Gods Must Be Crazy*. The story is about an empty pop bottle falling from an airplane somewhere in a remote village in Africa. The people of the village knew nothing about glass or soft drink bottles. When they found the bottle, they viewed it as a gift from the gods that rode in the great noisy birds (airplanes). In their belief system there were no referent ideas for airplanes or pop bottles. The nearest this foreign object came to fitting into their belief system and language was as a gift from the gods.

People in the village began to treasure the bottle. New emotions such as jealousy and violence erupted. After months of turmoil, they finally sent a man to throw it off the edge of the world and return it to the gods. The bottle fit into their belief system in ways that were harmful to the villagers. The new emotions were dangerous and they chose to remove the source of the problem. Another choice would have been to change the meaning of the bottle so it had little or no emotional charge. They might have viewed it as a danger and buried it far away from the village.

Ingrained in each belief is an emotional charge. We always have the option of choosing our attitude or emotional charge in reaction to any situation thereby adjusting the belief. If you feel angry and defiant, you may clench your fist, plant your feet firmly or tighten your jaw and stomach muscles. If you are recalling the situation, your body may tense slightly. Along with an emotional charge, each belief expresses itself with facial and bodily expressions.

Our bodies reflect our emotions. If we find ourselves in difficulty or danger, we tense and brace to flee or do battle. The adrenaline and norepinephrine levels rise. Our minds prepare physical defense and attack strategies. Our heart races and our breathing rate increases. We become highly alert and energized.

We express beliefs, attitudes and emotions on subtle levels starting before birth. Therapists now believe that at birth a baby has a framework of belief that is sent by hormones and is shared between mother and child while the child is still in the womb. This framework of belief also includes the sounds that make up spoken words. The fetus picks up and reacts to these sounds.

After birth, we take on some nonverbal beliefs of our parents and siblings. Of course, we can't question these beliefs. We don't possess the verbal skills to question anything. We use these early nonverbal beliefs as the basic framework for our later beliefs. As infants, we fill this framework with verbal belief as best we can as our word skills develop.

We have all experienced discovering that we believed something was ridiculous, but with our level of reasoning skill it was the closest we could come to understanding at the time. This understanding somehow fit into our framework of belief. Santa Claus is a good example. I wonder how much of what we experience is the result of filling our framework of reality with the prejudices of our beliefs and physical senses? How can the world outside be different to us than the world we represent to ourselves inside? How can the outside world ever be as large as the inside world?

As adults, we can reach these nonverbal beliefs easier through bodily feeling and emotions. Many of these beliefs were formed before we could talk. We usually find it difficult to think about them especially if they are threatening. Sometimes it's helpful to discover the circumstances that formed the belief. If our beliefs were formed as a result of an earlier trauma, it may be desirable or even necessary to relive the memory of the trauma in order to adjust the belief and release the related stress. At times, you must express the pain or emotion associated with a belief to allow yourself to release the belief.

To begin the healing you only need awareness of the belief with the intent to change it. This awareness may come on a nonverbal level such as your energy patterns, physical stance or emotional charge. Sometimes you may have to express the intent on more than one level to update a belief pattern. You may express intent by words, actions, emotions, physical stance, attitudes, willpower or artistic expression.

All beliefs consist of supporting beliefs. No single belief stands alone. Each belief exists in its own environment and is altered by any change in supporting beliefs.

Before you can believe that you can run you must believe that you can stand and walk. You must also believe that running is possible. If you injure a knee and believe that you can no longer walk without a cane, you won't believe you can still run and you may never try running again.

Every belief about your ability to move your body is altered by the belief you can walk only with a cane. Until you prove to yourself that you can run again, you are burdened with a limited belief about running.

Loss of Soul Exercise

I invite you now to find a comfortable position and begin to settle into your body, becoming aware of whatever supports you, what you're resting on. Feeling gravity, allowing gravity to support you, knowing gravity won't fail you. Just relaxing into that knowledge, that assurance, that trust. Begin to scan your body and take inventory of what's going on right now. Checking in on all your extremities. Checking in on the bone marrow as well as the hard outer layer of the bone. All through your torso and internal organs. All the muscles of your body. All the space that is inside your body.

And, as you continue to settle in your body, we're going to explore a bit. Realize, in your daily life you expend a certain amount of energy. If you were to consider all of this energy as a full tank of gas, notice now where you use this energy. What burns up your gas? Starting first thing in the morning and proceeding through your day, just notice where you invest your energy. Notice how much of your gas is consumed by thinking. Notice the quality of these thoughts. Are they productive thoughts? Are they obsessive thoughts? Do they help you in your daily life? Or do they run you down? Notice if one kind of thought takes more energy than another.

When you perform a task in life, how much energy is used by thinking, worrying, telling yourself that it's too hard and why should I have to be the one to do it anyway?

And how much of your energy is used in the actual task of doing it. Just notice, no judgment, nothing to do about it. Just notice. Notice now how much of your gas for the day or energy for the day is invested in other people? How much of your energy do you put into maintaining other people's lives? And how much energy do you put into your possessions? And notice how much of your energy, when you have done all the other things of the day, is left for fulfilling your life, for getting what you want in life. Just notice.

Now bring your awareness to your life challenge. Notice how much of your daily energy is invested in your life challenge. Notice how much of this energy is invested in your relationship with your life challenge, how you feel about it and how you interact with it in your daily life. And notice how much of your energy is used up by the relationship between your life challenge and the world. Notice how much of the energy that's invested in your life challenge is used for healing that life challenge, for changing it in a healthier way . . . for moving toward that state that is health for you, whatever that may be. Just notice without judgment. Take as much time as you choose to really explore the things that you have discovered . . . to make any changes that you feel are appropriate.

Take all the time you choose, and when you are ready, just let your eyes open and your consciousness return to the room around you.

Reclaiming Your Energy Exercise

Take a couple of deep breaths. Just release the tension each time you exhale. Settle into your body and begin to just relax. Wherever you're at right now take a moment to adjust yourself into a truly comfortable position. Feel your

breath moving deeper and deeper into your body. Allow
your breath to move into your belly now, your belly is
expanding with each inhale and contracting with each
exhalation. Feeling the deliciousness of the sensations as
the breath moves through your body . . . letting your breath
move into your pelvis now. Expanding like the bulb of an
eyedropper. Expanding at your hips and the front and back
of your pelvis and your pelvic floor. Expanding with each
inhalation. Contracting with each exhalation—as if squeezing the bulb of the eyedropper. Letting your breath move
down through your legs to the bottoms of your feet. Moving
into your arms and hands. Filling your neck and head. Your
entire skin expanding with each inhalation. Contracting
with each exhalation. Feeling your skin as a single unit,
flexible and strong, covering your entire body. And as you
move through your daily life, you invest your energy in
many areas: people, places, ideas, things. You expend you
energy in these ways.

I'd like to invite you, now, to notice the part of your body
where you connect to the people in your life . . . maybe it's
many parts. Just notice. Bring your awareness to your skin
at the places where you connect. Move your awareness
closer and closer into those places. Noticing now which
connections serve you in your life and which connections
drain you. And if you feel it's appropriate, just let go of
those places that drain you and seal them off so that they
can't connect to you again. Notice the places where you
connect to your possessions. Just bring your awareness to
those areas of your skin. I invite you to choose which of
these connections serve and which don't. If it's appropriate
disconnect from those that do not serve you and seal off the
place of connection so that it cannot be reattached to.
Follow your heart in these matters. Notice the place where
you choose to connect to ideas.

You can choose to let go of those ideas that no longer serve you, that no longer feel true inside, that are no longer nourishing. Just release them and seal off these places of connection and bring your awareness to your life challenge. Notice the place where it connects with you inside. Wherever appropriate, disconnect from it, withdraw your energy from it and seal those points of connection. Notice how your life challenge connects to the world. Bring your awareness to these places of connection and wherever appropriate, withdraw your energy, and seal the points of connection. Take all the time you choose to work with these connections. Disconnecting, reclaiming your energy and reassigning your life energy to being fulfilled as a person . . . to healing as a person . . . creating the life that you want, that you choose . . . that you desire inside.

Take all the time you choose to work with these connections. When you're ready allow your eyes to open and your consciousness to return to the room around you.

Community Mind

We infuse our relationships, ideas and beliefs, and material things with our life energy. In a way, we become attached to these things and maintain them as living entities with our energy. This is similar to the way we infuse a trauma with our life energy and envelop it in the body to create an inner child. It's like a complex web of energy exists both inside and outside of our bodies. We have an invisible brain that connects by energetic pathways to other people, memories and things. When a person infuses a belief, all people in their unique way who share that belief unconsciously and automatically infuse that same belief. This becomes the community mind.

The action of community mind is seen in the insect and animal kingdoms. The efficient team work in ants and bees is well-known. When building a place to live or defending the colony there is only a single mind operating. When a flock of geese fly, they form a vee formation to break the wind and conserve energy. There is no set leader of the flock. The lead position is constantly being filled by a different bird from the flock. The whole flock operates as a single mind. As humans we are influenced by the common mind of our family and society. In any given setting, we can usually tell how acceptable we are without having to ask anyone. We tend to unconsciously adjust ourselves to fit in. This relationship with the larger mind influences our stress level and therefore our health.

Most people in our society share a belief in chairs. If you place a chair in a huge hall and bring in a thousand people to view the chair, each person sees a chair. But, some see a comfortable chair, others see an antique chair, some see a wooden chair and so on. Each view is personal and different.

It's as though we go through life with many invisible bubbles attached to our bodies. Like cartoon dialogue bubbles, each bubble contains the potential for emotions, beliefs and experiences. When we meet people, they offer several cartoon bubbles that might be shared. You may then join in their belief, emotion or action bubble. You, as well, offer them your bubbles to join with or reject. Upon connecting with one of these bubbles, each person expresses interests in his or her way.

At times you might notice that as you pass someone, thoughts that don't seem right just pop into your head. For example, you might see someone and think that she is a friendly person. Yet the thought, this person has a big nose and is unworthy, crosses your mind. You didn't even notice her nose or have any feelings about noses. You unknowingly joined her bubble of belief. She offered you the bubble that contains abuse over nose size. If you also feel anxious about the size of your nose, you immediately join her bubble. You may each feel distaste toward the other because of nose size and hurry on your way. Or, you may become defensive and verbally attack her before she can attack you. Or, you may become friends because of the instant recognition that you are both attached to the nasal abuse bubble.

These bubbles of potential are one aspect of the community or universal mind. When you infuse these bubbles with your awareness or life energy, you suffer what a shaman might call, loss of soul. In the Ayurvedic practice they say this is forgetting your divine or universal nature. Psychotherapists call this "having poor boundaries."

An example of loss of soul was explained to me by a friend. It was her way of coping in the world. She said, "It's like I have these things I worry about all around me," motioning to her waist to show the worries as being attached to her by strings. "When the stress from worrying about one thing becomes overwhelming, I just start worrying about something else. I kind of move around my waist from one set of worries to another." This is loss of soul because it drains her life energy.

This is a source of constant and sometimes extreme stress and anxiety in her daily life. She uses most of her energy supporting her circle of worries. The overflowing bags of churning emotion hanging from her waist are carried with her weighing her down and sapping her energy. Life for her is tiring and difficult.

By the shared beliefs, the community mind sets the limits or boundaries of acceptable behavior and experience. Each nerve ending in the body is attached to a Schwann cell. These cells also exist at every point of connection between the spine and nervous system. There is evidence Schwann cells act as transceivers that relay information throughout the body by a direct current energy field. Like a radio transmitter and receiver, Dr. Becker and other researchers think you can pick up this field of radio-like signals from other people's bodies. In this way, firsthand knowledge of the inner workings of other people's minds and bodies may be available to you. We have mentioned the communication that seems to exist between all life on a DNA level. These subtle, direct current signals may be the source of the community mind. The community mind is also called the universal mind or the Akashic Records.

Vibrant Truth

When working with PNI, we work with vibrant truths. Vibrant truth is when we use imaginary people, creatures or things along with real medicine and treatments. For example, the little boy mentioned earlier helped his brain tumor disappear by imagining white space ships that flew around and zapped the tumor with space rays. In actual reality this is totally inaccurate. Yet in its essence and effects, it is true, accurate and effective. Like the virtual reality produced by clever computer software, the spaceships are in the computer's (boy's) memory, however, their effects are real. We have no white spaceships in our brains. But there are white blood cells and macrophages that move through the blood and act like spaceships with laser rays.

The Russians have done extensive research with biophotons. These biophotons are beams of light which each cell appears to emit on all measurable wavelengths. The space-type rays the boy used may be biophotons even though he did not know the actual working physiology of his immune system. But, he knew his immune system on an intuitive level and represented it to himself in images he could understand. His story was beyond the grasp of his doctors and beyond his knowledge to say what was actually happening.

It isn't nearly as important to understand how your body functions in a scientific, medical way. What is important is to bring your awareness to the problem and express your intent to heal on a level that you understand. Sometimes intellect can be the biggest barrier to effective action.

The Silent Witness

In cases of multiple personalities it is common for the different personalities to have different physical ailments. One personality may have allergies that disappear when another personality takes over. One personality may be diabetic while another in the same body is not. Sometimes the blood type changes with a change of personalities. This supports the idea that mind and body are a whole unit and you can't change one without changing the other.

One personality, in cases of multiple personality disorder, often refers to itself; "the one who was born with this body and the one who will continue after this body is laid down." This is the silent witness that retains consciousness during surgery or in a coma. Your silent witness is the part of you that is awake during sleep and the part that reaches out in the world to warn you of danger.

The presence of the silent witness is dramatically illustrated by two young boys, Roger and Jeff. Roger was three years old when I began working with him. He weighed less than one pound at birth. Doctors said he was no more than a vegetable. They thought him to be deaf, blind and without voluntary brain function. When I first worked with Roger it was on the pretext of doing therapeutic touch/unruffling (see pages 132-133) in hopes he could go through a holiday season without pneumonia. I began to probe his soft body energy with my hands as I unruffled the energy layers. Soon, I gently cradled the back of his head in my hands as I connected heart to heart with him. I felt a flash of emotion as he and I made contact between our silent witnesses. Roger began to cry, something he hadn't done before unless he was in extreme physical pain. Yet, this time it seemed as if he noticed other life existed for the first time and he wasn't alone. His cries seemed a mixture of joy, sadness, hope and loneliness. Since then Roger is more aware of his family, and they feel he knows they are around. He also made it through the holidays without pneumonia for the first time and continues to grow healthier. He now attends a special school where he seems to enjoy being in the circle when games are being played. He responds to the touch and presence of other children.

The other boy, Jeff, was about ten and facing two long, difficult back operations to install steel rods along his spine. Before the surgeries, we spent only a short time together. We had very little time to work. What seemed most important and potentially dangerous, as I understood it, was the extreme blood loss that might occur. We focused most of our time on teaching him to stay partially conscious and monitor the amount of blood lost. I suggested different ways Jeff might control the blood loss and keep the area where the surgery was taking place free of blood that might hinder the progress of the operations. I suggested he could draw the blood away from the operations by imagining it being blocked from getting to the area. He used images of his blood vessels constricting to squeeze off the blood flow, his heart beating slower and his body becoming colder.

I suggested that his silent witness could be aware of the operations to watch for complications to prevent them before they happened. I offered these suggestions to Jeff while he was in a deep hypnotic state. After the actual operations the surgeon said that they were the best surgeries he had ever done. He said it was as if something or someone had been guiding him. The blood loss during both operations was about half the amount they predicted.

In both boys, it seems as if they contacted some greater aspect and this greater aspect began to take an active role in their healing.

Awareness and Intent

We have a cat named Spunky. Spunky has bladder problems caused by seafood. Crystals form in his bladder and clog it so much he can't urinate. He came close to death several times before he (the cat) learned how to manage his problem including adjusting what he ate and the person who fed him. The first time he got sick the veterinarian prescribed pills to keep the crystals from forming. Spunky hates pills. He is an amiable cat in most situations, unless he's being given medicine, then we have to wrap him in a towel to control him long enough for him to take his pill. He became very good at pretending to swallow the pill, but we would find it later on the floor or under the couch. When he took his pills every day he was all right, but because of his slyness, we didn't know if he was swallowing them.

Spunky learned quickly that seafood caused his problems and simply quit eating the troublesome seafood. With this awareness came a natural intent that led him to take the right action to solve his bladder problem and keep him alive. But that wasn't enough. He still got sick.

Spunky is a good cat. He seldom jumps on counters or begs. Most of the time he is tolerant and dignified. Suddenly, however, he began jumping on the counter or the table. At first we were puzzled since he's not usually eager to eat. He raised quite a ruckus until he found what he needed to dissolve the crystals. Asparagus! It took him only a few days to train Anna, my wife, to prepare three asparagus spears for him every day. He never lets her forget and he doesn't have bladder problems anymore. We stopped giving him any medicine.

The intelligence essential for knowing a life challenge is very primitive. Spunky discovered his life challenge, found what caused it and came up with a solution. His intent was to heal himself. He didn't want to die. He gained guidance from the life challenge and took corrective action based on this guidance *The Spunky Factor*. The difference between Spunky and a human with a similar condition is that Spunky lacked an emotional agenda or limiting beliefs to attach to his life challenge. He simply chose health and proceeded to heal himself. As people, we have hidden and unconscious conditioning that we bring to healing. There are usually secondary gains in being sick such as knowing we only get the touching and intimacy we need when sick. Old beliefs set limits: "My mother, grandmother and great-grandmother had gall stones and I will get them" or "Cancer is incurable and even if I survived I would always be in pain anyway." There are underlying emotional stressors that cause a continuous low level panic. When we consider a life challenge, we must address all the aspects we discover, and we must be open to seeing beyond our beliefs.

Awareness and intent are the essential dynamics in all human creation. We intend that something happens in our world and in the act of intending we cause an awareness that leads to actions to reach our goals. If we follow this guidance by taking the right action, we can reach our reasonable goals. A reasonable goal is one that fits within the boundaries of our belief system.

Cybernetics, the study of electromechanical control systems, describes the physical process of intending an outcome such as grasping a glass of water. We make many adjustments until the glass is in hand. This is an unconscious process that happens with such speed that we can't think of every movement. Imagine how difficult it would be to get a drink of water if you had to think through each step of the process. How long would it take you to notice and coordinate each muscle and its interaction with the other muscles, nerves and body systems. These adjustments are automatic in practice.

Psychocybernetics is the same adjustment process on a psychological level. Most actions in life can be compared to piloting a sailboat. While under sail, the boat is off course more than ninety percent of the time. The pilot makes many minor adjustments to arrive at his destination. If he makes no adjustments, he won't arrive at his planned destination.

In every action, if you intend an outcome and you bring your intent, energy and awareness to the situation, you will automatically find guidance. If you take the action directed by your awareness, you will eventually produce your reasonable goal. You will reach your planned destination even if you take the wrong action since you make adjustments along the way. Even with mistakes, you move ever closer to your goal. If you don't take the appropriate action, you may not reach your goal. Like sailing a boat, the only mistake is not to adjust your actions according to your guidance.

You may not have time to think about the corrective

action. If you put your hand on something hot, you immediately pull your hand away without thinking. Nothing told you verbally to move your hand, but there was a guidance to move it. You wouldn't think of resisting this inner guidance then, but often you have learned to ignore your nonverbal inner guidance in favor of belief or thoughts.

Some people believe that the challenges they have in life are lessons they must learn, as if they were punishment. These challenges are lessons in the sense that they provide an opportunity to learn from the results of your intentions and actions.

You can use this feedback to adjust your actions to create the desired outcome. To think of them as self-imposed or divinely ordained punishment is not productive. Such attitudes create guilt that only serves as a catalyst for more stress and barriers in your life.

You experience what you believe. Nothing exists within your reality that you do not believe in. Your belief system is the result of your intent in life. In all aspects of life you hold certain beliefs in favor of other beliefs. If, for example, you are a burglar, you then choose the belief that it's all right to steal. Your belief matches your intent. If you're the victim of the burglary, you will choose the belief that it is unlawful to steal. Again, your belief matches your intent. If you believe you cannot heal a life challenge, then your intent to heal is limited by that belief. You interfere with any healing process.

You must define healing in your way. One person with cancer might find that healing for him is complete remission with no scars. Another person's healing might be to accept himself and the things he did during his life. Only you can know what healing means to you. It's likely that this knowing will be nonverbal. To help define your healing, you might find inspiration in a feeling, a dream, a vision, a song, a sound in nature or from another aspect of your life.

True healing on a personal level is living a life of richness in relationships and experiences. Moving toward a life that fulfills you as a person, regardless of where you must start, the amount of time you have or the life challenges that you may encounter on your journey, is a process of healing. At the end of your life you will die like everyone else. When you have reached the end of this life's journey, the only real healing is to let go of your body to continue your journey. All great mystics, healers and gurus die. Most die from the same causes as people in general. Some die in extreme pain from cancer. Although, they have a different relationship with the pain and cancer than most people. They savor the wonder of life and embrace each moment in a celebration of life. Anything that moves you toward being truly alive now, in my opinion, is healing. Only you can know what this healing is for you.

Awareness and intent are key psychoneuroimmunology (PNI) techniques. The most direct technique in sharing in one's own healing is to simply bring awareness to the challenge with the intent that you heal. Bringing awareness with intent is the required first action in causing anything to happen. If you only wish a thing without taking action, or fail to make continual adjustment, you likely won't get results. All techniques start with intent. You suddenly notice a dark, uneven growth on your skin. The longer you choose to ignore it, the more damage will occur if it turns out to be a malignant melanoma. The longer you ignore the growing pain alerting you to the advancing damage from cancer, the more advanced the cancer will be when you allow yourself to recognize it. At this point, your very survival is at stake. The longer you wait to begin treatment the more the damage done to you physically, emotionally, intellectually and spiritually. It's easy to see how having cancer might cause a person to change beliefs, have many different emotions and reassess spiritual relationships. It is also easy to see why it's important to do so.

Precious Pain

The way we develop our early relationship with pain is easy to see. If you have ever seen a toddler fall and bump his head while his mother is watching, assuming the fall wasn't traumatic enough to cause terror, you have seen him get up and look to his mother to see how she was reacting. If she doesn't pay attention to him, he gets up and continues as if nothing much happened. If he sees his mother gasp and hold her breath, he will gasp and hold his breath and begin to cry. Until he learns otherwise, pain is just a sensation of the moment and won't be given much notice unless it's extreme or accompanied by fear.

I remember learning about pain and suffering as a child. At age six, I smashed my finger in a mountain climbing accident. I had to wear a cast on my finger for what seemed like months. The cast was a nuisance, but overall it was not something that held my awareness. The tumble down the mountain, the falling rock and multiple cuts were terrifying to me, but the only real pain I remember was the shot in the rear given by the doctor. Even that was a strange sensation which made one buttock feel heavier than the other.

Not long after the accident I was playing in the yard and an older neighbor boy came up to me and said, "I'll bet you're in a lot of pain."

"Pain?" I replied puzzled. "What's pain?"

I knew hurt, but this pain was a little different somehow. The neighbor boy, who normally wouldn't talk to me because I was so much younger, explained pain to me and acted like my friend since I had so much of this pain stuff. He taught me that there was virtue in suffering. This changed my relationship with pain completely from a simple signal that something needed attending to something of value that could be exploited. During early childhood is the period of brain development when that portion of the brain which associates with the ability to suffer with pain is becoming fully activated. This portion is called the neomammalian complex.

Pain can guide us to maximum health and healing. Pain is precious guidance and you should not try to take pain away completely. It may be desirable to reduce pain to a level of comfort that allows you to be open to its guidance. If you break your leg, some pain is useful to remind you that you have a serious injury and need to allow ample time for healing before playing sports again. If you had no pain, you would probably not take care of yourself or allow yourself to heal properly. Your leg might even deteriorate to the point where you would never be able to walk normally again. Even small, subtle pain can tell you something. We often confuse pain and suffering. Although they often occur at the same time, one has little to do with the other. Pain is a simple sensory signal of the state of your body or emotions. The part of your brain that processes physical pain is the same part that processes emotional pain. To the brain the two are the same. Awareness must be brought to the pain to be able to isolate the two. Suffering is the verbal and emotional process we go through when we are in pain. Suffering depends on belief.

If you simply keep your awareness with any pain sensations, the larger aspects of the sensation will begin to present themselves. It's as if you see through the eyes of another person. You step into that part of your personality causing the sensations. These sensations might be pain, itching, muscle tightness or any other body signals. This is the basis behind body-centered psychotherapies such as Integral Therapy. Thus, a most effective route to healing or changing, is to intend the change and bring the awareness to your body. Your body has many potential healing talents not yet known to modern science. We know instinctively, if not consciously, how to operate our bodies. Our increasing awareness results in increasing ability to direct and control our world.

Because of the construction of the human brain, we can begin to understand why emotional and physical pain are inseparable. The human brain is made up of three main levels or brains. The job of the brain stem or reptilian complex is to maintain basic life support, sexual drive and to tell us to run from danger. The awareness of the reptilian brain is limited to the physical world of daily survival and yet all nerve circuitry to higher brain levels passes through the brain stem. If the emotional affairs of the old mammalian brain cause pain, that pain is detected by the brain stem and represented in the only way possible as physical pain. Any physical pain you feel has a counterpart in emotions and reason. Even if the wound is purely physical, such as a broken leg, there is also an emotional charge. You may feel stupid for having followed the ski patrol through terrain you weren't skilled enough to be on and humiliated when they had to bring you down the mountain on a stretcher. This is certainly emotional pain. To soothe the emotional pain that compounds the physical pain, you may tell yourself that it's all the fault of the snow groomers on the other side of the mogul who neglected to cover the rock which you hit, consequently, breaking your leg. This compounds the pain again by adding the psychological pain of blaming someone else and thereby choosing to be a victim.

You might react to the psychological pain by choosing the belief that you are inadequate, and it is therefore God's fault that you broke your leg. God must not love you, so you react in anger—now adding another source of pain to the injury. There really is no separation in this process. All occur at the same time. The different ways the layers of your brain are able to represent the world are some of the different ways that you naturally represent your worlds to yourselves. The pain in your body serves to make you aware that you need to stop the emotional reactions and focus on how to do to deal with the broken leg. You have the ability to bring your awareness to your leg and see what unfulfilled need it is alerting you to. As with hunger, you check with the feeling and you know what you are hungry for, at least on a physical level. If there is an emotional hunger that you are trying to fill, food won't fulfill the need. You will have to keep your awareness with the hunger sensation a little longer to discover the emotional hunger. If you keep trying to feed this hunger with food, it will keep coming back and you may never be satisfied.

With the emotional charge there will be a belief system that supports it. If the emotional charge is the need for love, the accompanying belief would be, "I am not lovable or there is no love available for me." Pain works the same way. If you are going to discover the emotional, physical and spiritual aspect of pain, you will have to keep your awareness with the pain long enough to allow it to reveal itself. If you have judgements about the pain or yourself for having the pain, you will probably block yourself from having the clarity to discover more about it. In most cases, the pain represents a part of yourself you don't accept. By itself, nonjudgmental acceptance of the pain will take you far in your healing. It's very important to note that acceptance is not the same as giving up. Acceptance is the practical action of honestly assessing where you are right now and what you need to do to get where you want to be. Giving up is quitting the path of knowing oneself.

Inspection Tour

I'd like to invite you now to go on a tour of your body. On this tour, if you find anything that doesn't feel right, that isn't getting proper nourishment, that needs repair or increased waste disposal, you can create helpers to keep the work in progress as you continue. These helpers can call on any other part of your body to nurture the healing process. They can call for support from other parts of your body. And there's a greater consciousness inside that knows how to heal. I invite you to trust that guidance to find your own healing. Healing and cure are very different things. Only you can decide what healing means to you. And the most reliable guide, to finding that healing and making it your own, is the guidance you find inside. So I invite you to trust that guidance as we begin this journey.

Let's begin this inspection tour with the skin. Your skin is the largest organ of your body and the most sensitive. Your skin contains you and keeps you from leaking out. It also protects you by letting in what you need to nourish you. Yet, it keeps out things that can harm you. Your skin is a membrane and it can choose what to let in and what to let out. A lot of waste is washed out through your skin and yet the water can't penetrate it to get inside your body. Your skin is waterproof. Just go over every square inch of your skin and notice how well it's containing you, how well it's protecting you. Are you too thin skinned? Do things that are toxic get through your skin? Do you leak outward? Is your skin too thick? So thick that it doesn't allow the nourishment in or the toxins to escape? If there are places where your skin leaks, leave some helpers to repair it. If you're too thin skinned, begin to make your skin thicker. If it's too thick make it thinner, whatever feels right. Only you can really know what's right for you.

Leave your helpers in charge of the various projects working with your skin. Continue now to your bones. Your skeletal system is the hardest part of your body. It's what makes it possible for you to stand up. And yet your bones are not really that solid. They're constantly changing. Just notice now if your bones are hard and shiny on the outside. Are they thick enough? Are they getting the nutrition they need? If not, send out messages to the proper places in your body to obtain any nutrition you need for your bones. Notice if your skeleton feels solid, like a single unit. Is your bone marrow healthy? Is it receiving all the materials it needs to perform its functions, like building white blood cells. And are the waste products being properly washed away. If there's anything to be improved, go ahead and create those helpers needed to carry on the work while you continue to your muscles.

Scan the muscles in your body. Notice any places that they might be stressed or damaged. Begin repairs in those places. Notice if they're in proper working condition. Are they properly exercised? Are they getting proper nutrition? Are they getting enough water? And are the wastes being washed away? Are they tense or relaxed? Are there any knots in your muscles? Do they have what they need to build new muscle? Are they coordinating properly with your nervous system and your sensory systems? Begin whatever repairs are needed. If they're not getting enough blood, increase the blood flow. Clean out the blood pathways. Whatever's proper now, just do it.

And bring your awareness now to your heart. Is it clean

and healthy? Is it damaged? Is it clogged up? Whatever needs to be done, begin the work. Create the necessary helpers. Follow the blood throughout your body. Is your blood healthy? Does it have everything it needs? Is it being properly cleaned? Is it getting enough oxygen and giving enough oxygen to the rest of the body? Is it performing all it's functions properly? Whatever's right, just begin to make those changes. Create the helpers and move on.

Bring your awareness to your lungs. Are they working properly? Are they exchanging oxygen and waste gases properly? Are they in good repair? Are they soft and supple? Whatever is needed here just go ahead and do it and move to your kidneys. Are they working properly, removing wastes from your body? Are they working in harmony with your glands? And are your hormones working in harmony with the rest of your body? Are your lymph glands swollen? Cleanse any impurities from your lymph glands. Whatever's proper, do it now and move from your lymphatic system to your nervous system.

Are your neural pathways clear so that information can pass freely? Are the nerve endings clear, clean and alive? Is there damage? The insulation might be cracked or missing. Possibly the nerve endings are traumatized. Just experience how your nervous system connects your brain with the rest of your body. It's as if the nerve endings were the controls that operate your body. Your brain is your onboard computer. Notice how all this is working. Is there any problem you need to understand? All you need to do is create the helpers with the intent that they fix it or repair it, that they bring it into a balance that creates the condition you call health.

Create those helpers now and start the process. Just let your awareness come to your mouth and notice that starting at your mouth there's a tunnel that goes all the way through your body and even though it's inside your body, it's also outside your body. As things pass through this tunnel your body takes what it needs to nourish it. Then, it lets what it doesn't need pass on through to be washed away, to be carried away in your daily eliminations. Just begin a journey now starting with your mouth and notice if everything is working properly. If it isn't, you can begin repairs before you move on to your throat and on to your stomach. Notice if the proper chemicals and enough water are available for proper digestion. Notice if the proper nutrients are being absorbed. Notice if there's any damage. Whatever you find, take the proper action to move toward better health. Absorbing more as you move through your small intestines doing the finer digestion. Moving on through your large intestine digesting more and more. If there's anything that needs repair or if there's anything that there is too much of or too little of, send out your messengers to obtain any help or material needed for balancing and making repairs. Move on. Notice the organs of elimination, the bladder, the colon, rectum and anus. If anything isn't working right or anything is in need of repair, call on the proper parts of your body to do whatever is needed, to obtain the necessary material or assistance. Create the needed helpers and move on.

Move now to your sexual organs, your organs for making another life. If there's anything that needs to be done here, create the helpers, call for the necessary support and move on.

Check your sinuses and ears. Your sensory capabilities and any other part of your body that has been overlooked. Take all the time you need to go back through your body to inventory the changes you have chosen. Double check with your helpers to be certain there's no misunderstanding. Take all the time you need. When you're ready, allow your eyes to open and your consciousness to return to the room around you.

Sensitivity Cycle

Ron Kurtz in *Body-Centered Psychotherapy, The Hakomi Method* describes the process of awareness and intent in daily life as the Sensitivity Cycle. He says that, first, there is a stage of *relaxation* where you drop your outside world view and begin to reorient to your internal needs. You notice what you need or want, now, and find *clarity* in your innate guidance. For example, you relax and realize that you are hungry. You check inside and find that you are hungry for rice and beans and not cake.

Next comes *effective* action. You're aware of what your body needs, you have identified what is necessary to fill that need and now you act to get it. When you have eaten the rice and beans, you have reached *satisfaction*, the last stage of the sensitivity cycle. Now you may relax, reorient to what you now need or want and start the cycle again. If you fail to complete any of the stages, hunger and nourishment aren't satisfied, and you become stuck in that stage until it is satisfied.

In the physical healing process we see the same dynamics in action. The metaphoric and sensory symbolic language of the unconscious mind has become fairly well-defined by modern behavioral science. The practice of hypnosis has developed the use of hypnotic language patterns and symbolic language of the subconscious mind in the same way that semanticists and linguists have studied the power of metaphor and language for centuries and given it symbolic language. Each person relates to the world with a unique blend of symbolism that includes sound, vision, speech, emotion and bodily sensations. Using the individual's own symbolism, it's easy to lead him to choose a new intent and continue the sensitivity cycle toward his own healing.

For example, if a person has trouble with anger and blanks out language and only sees the red light of rage, it is better to focus on seeing the redness of rage than to talk about the virtue of not losing your temper. Stepping into the experience makes its attributes available now. In rage without words, change becomes easier when dealt with as highly intense images, feelings or bodily sensations. Like learning to ride a bike, you can talk about it forever and still you can't ride until you get on the bike and practice several times.

Most people require some form of symbolism, at first, to deliver the intent and to process the awareness or innate guidance. The symbols help to maintain concentration and focus. The symbolic form makes no difference. A person may be naturally more inclined to imagery, meditation, sound, movement, feeling or other method. All symbols are the result of preverbal experience and as such always reflect the vibrational truth of the person's state of being. What we experience is registered truthfully and accurately while being stored in different symbols. It's when we translate experience into words that we rapidly lose truth and accuracy. As you learn to move farther away from the verbal description of the event to the actual feelings, you become more accustomed to being present and not two steps removed from the event in a world of talk.

When you work with imagery, in the language of Milton Erickson and neurolinguistic programmers, you are in essence accessing resource states. For example, if in a hypnotic state you are given the suggestion that wind is blowing through a wart on your hand, the image will probably cause an increase in blood oxygen to the area of the wart. The wart may begin to disappear if you are not unconsciously hanging onto the wart because of a belief such as "I am ugly and deserve to have warts." Of course this belief, like all beliefs, has an emotional charge that goes along with it. The wart may be the result of the stress created by the belief you are ugly.

If you have been caught in a tornado and are terrified of wind, this suggestion might cause the opposite effect by contracting the muscles and decreasing the oxygen in the area of the wart. In each case the way you hold your life energy is different. The principles of therapeutic touch state that energy always follows thought; physical form always follows energetic form. Kirlian photography shows that before a plant grows a new leaf the energetic outline of the leaf appears and then the energy field fills into the actual leaf.

You can change the energy phase, energy being a precursor to matter, of the situation by simply bringing awareness to the wart with the intent that it go away. If there is an overwhelming emotional charge and the real intent toward this wart is that it exist, it won't go away. If you are willing to let go of the belief system or the emotional charge (a defensive mechanism), then the wart disappears. It isn't easy to give up your defenses unquestioned.

The use of imagery is the use of intent and awareness. When you intend an outcome, you begin to become aware of the situation and the possible action which you need to take to create the outcome. If you take effective action, you move closer to your goal. If you take an ineffective action, you learn it doesn't work and you move on to another plan of action. Your intent takes you to possible actions. Within the action is the intent. The intent becomes the guidance that brings the awareness of the need to change the plan of action or intent. Intent and awareness aren't separate events or entities. They are intellectual markers in the procession of life. They are the two sides of the flipping coin and cannot exist separately.

A Matter of Balance

All things are in a state of constantly shifting balance. The universe is in an organic balance that keeps the movement of stars, planets, galaxies and superclusters in harmony. The orbit of each planet in our solar system is balanced and held in its orbit by the motion of the other planets and their moons as they revolve around the sun. In a similar way, subatomic particles hold each other in a balanced orbit to make up the structure of each atom. Atoms hold each other in balanced motion to construct molecules. These systems of balance permeate every aspect of our lives. We live under the influence of political balances of power on individual, family, local, state, national, ecological and international levels. We have seen, in family therapy, how each member of the family compensates for (or balances) the other members. The chemical balances in your body seem endless.

This system of balance exists on a personal level, as well. Some personal balances that influence healing are physical, intellectual, emotional and spiritual. Each balance, from the smallest subatomic particle to the largest supercluster in the universe, affects all other balances as shown by chaos physics. The working balances of your body—instant to instant—are influenced by the system of constantly changing balances inside and outside yourself. So, the balances that compose your entire being interact with and balance with the greater and smaller balances of the universe.

PNI works on the assumption that a person may consciously influence the balances within and that they may choose to interact with the inside and the outside worlds in a way that isn't harmful. Stress may be the cause of growth or regression depending on how you react to it. This implies we can choose how to understand and interact with the outside world and the ability to choose our attitude in any situation.

We have the capacity to change simply by intending change to happen and taking action to move toward it. In the 1960's, Fritz Perls said that awareness is curative in itself. Ron Kurtz believes in organicity or the innate capacity of all life to heal itself. Kurtz believes people have the capacities necessary to heal any given problem, discomfort or disease according to what is appropriate to their healing. If you intend to heal, your awareness begins to bring into your consciousness the necessary action to cause that healing. The intent guides the awareness that guides the intent. It is a self-fulfilling cycle that continues until altered by a conflicting belief or emotional charge.

This system of balances, that make up you, may be changed by making changes in any aspect of the total balance. You can use any aspect of your existence to cause changes in other aspects.

Expansion and Contraction Exercise

I'd like to invite you now to bring your awareness into your body and begin to experience your skin as the single incredibly sensitive organ that it is. Bring your awareness to where it just barely fills your body as if your skin was clear plastic and your awareness was water. Just fill your skin with that awareness. Begin to bring that awareness into your torso. Let your awareness move down just into your heart, becoming the size of your heart. Now, let your awareness grow to the size of a golf ball. The size of a marble, the size of a pea. Continuing on down to the size of a single cell. Shrinking smaller and smaller to the size of an atom. And now to the size of a subatomic particle, smaller than the smallest particle that makes up matter. Now shrinking to half that size and half that size again.

Now allow your awareness to grow larger, to the size of a subatomic particle. To the size of an atom and growing to the size of a single cell . . . a pea, a marble, a golf ball, the ·size of your heart. The size of your body, the size of the room you're in . . . the size of the building you're in. Growing to the size of the town you're in. And continuing to grow to the size of the state or country you are in and growing to the size of your continent . . . the size of your hemisphere . . . to the size of the earth, filling the earth's skin perfectly as if it were your own. Growing large enough now to include the moon and growing to the size of our solar system . . . to the size of our galaxy . . . the size of our galaxy cluster . . . growing to the size of the universe. All that exists. Now growing twice as large and doubling your size again.

Now begin to grow smaller to the size of the universe. Then to the size of our galaxy cluster . . . to the size of the milky way . . . to the size of our solar system . . . to the size of the earth . . . growing to the size of your hemisphere bringing your awareness back to the size of your continent . . . back to the size of your country . . . to the size of your town . . . to the size of the building you are in and growing back to the size of your skin. Filling your skin perfectly and fully.

Take all the time you choose to feel what you may be experiencing. When you're ready allow your eyes to open and your consciousness to return to the room around you.

Chapter 3

Four Realms of Healing

Many psychotherapists work within four realms to cause a shift toward healing—spiritual, emotional, intellectual and physical. These correspond to the energy-matter continuum as follows: energy to spirit, sound to emotion, light to intellect and matter to physical. All aspects are functions of energy as it vibrates at increasingly slower rates.

The easiest path to your life challenge is starting at the sensations in your body and following them through the realms of emotion, belief and energy (or spiritual) to the place where they begin. When changing your relationships with your life challenge, it's easier to work in the other direction. Changes made on an energetic level will affect all other levels. If resistance to these changes exists on the emotional, belief or physical levels, it may be proper to work on those levels as well. It's easier to change an emotional charge by altering the belief that supports it than to change it by curing the bodily symptoms. It's possible to change the emotional charge by working with the physical symptoms, but it's more efficient to work with the causes.

The sensations in your physical body create the map. The beliefs fill in the details. The emotion supplies the intent. Your relationship with the universe influences all of these.

Relationship

All aspects of the following realms of healing can be expressed as relationships. All aspects of your being are reflected by your relationships: interpersonal and intrapersonal.

Your soft body is like a pure energy potential that molds itself as defined by the influences and possibilities within your DNA, environment and psychological makeup. Intent determines which possibilities will be expressed and which will not. Another way of saying this is that intent is the choice of what will be infused with life energy (soft body) and what will not be infused by the same energy that gives life to our bodies. As a developing embryo you had the potential for expressing as any form of life on earth. Yet, you developed as a human expressing yourself with human features as opposed to flippers and hooves. This is the biological intent of our species.

Your relationships influence the way you infuse your body with energy. A relationship of anger may cause you to restrict energy flow in your body or cause it to stagnate in certain areas. Other relationships may cause you to lose or withdraw all but essential life energy from your body as a defense against fear or pain. All these things alter the flow of energy through your acupuncture meridians.

As humans, we are sensitive to the emotional charges of those around us. A metaphor for this process is through the example of a tuning fork. If you strike one tuning fork and bring it close to another tuning fork of the same frequency the second fork will begin to vibrate, even if it is of another octave. If you strike a C fork and bring it next to a C fork that is an octave higher or lower, it will still vibrate. This is called resonance. If you bring the same C fork next to a fork of any other frequency, even one only slightly different from C, the second fork won't vibrate. It doesn't resonate.

Emotions resonate in a similar way. For example, if someone you work with is yelled at by the boss, he or she may feel anger or shame. As a fellow human you will also feel anger or shame to the degree that you empathize with your co-worker. If the person is your friend, you will resonate more intensely with anger or shame than if the person is someone you don't like. Regardless of who it is, even if you don't know them or know that they were yelled at, you will resonate with them to some extent. If the strongest memory of anger or shame is being scolded as a child for stealing cookies, you may have a strange craving for cookies. As a matter of mental health, we develop defense mechanisms to lessen our resonance with others. Those who lose the ability to muffle the resonance tend to end up in mental institutions.

Recently, I demonstrated resonance to a college class. During the demonstration, a student started crying as she talked about a family member with cancer. Suddenly, she jumped up and ran from the room. Everyone in the room felt her intense emotion.

Another student asked, "Is that what you mean by resonance?"

"Yes," I affirmed.

In this opportune moment, I could have been used more fully if I had pointed out that everyone in the room had common reactions in our bodies. I could have pointed out that our breathing had moved to our upper chests while our bellies tightened. I might have brought awareness to the tightening each of us felt in our throats or the buildup of soft body energy in our chests. I might have had students notice whether memories of personal tragedies were streaming into their awareness. In the moment, I was resonating with her sorrow and fear. Like the others in the class, I felt like crying.

Imagine living in an environment where everyone around you is always angry. With anger, there is always fear. Anger and fear are common conditions in many families. If you live your life in anger, your body will bear the consequences of this constant stress. Anger tightens your jaw and neck. It concentrates soft body energy in your head where you run your angry thoughts. Your shoulders and back tighten and your heart rate and blood pressure increase meanwhile your breathing becomes restricted. Fight or flight hormones course through your body. When you walk into a room, everyone's neck and jaw tightens. They unconsciously react with defensive strategies like attacking you or ignoring you. This creates an internal environment that may result in any number of unpleasant bodily consequences.

Some people claim that you create your world and your life challenge. It is true that how you experience the world must fit into your belief system. Your world tends to stay consistent with your constant narration of your experience. When we resonate unchecked with the people around us, our thoughts and feelings are subject to the whims of anyone that comes near. When we are aware of this, we can begin to stop our resonance with others when we choose.

Relationship in healing can be as helpful as it can be harmful. I attended the first annual AIDS, Medicine and Miracles conference several years ago. Like most of the world at that time, I thought that all people who were HIV-positive developed full-blown AIDS and died within a year. I had never heard of long-term survivors, but at the conference there were some who had survived for as long as ten years. Many of the survivors seemed healthy. The thing that became clear as each long-term survivor spoke was that each one knew *why* they had survived. They had no doubt about it. They knew they had survived because they were in solid, supportive, loving relationships. They spoke about their mates using the same words that I had often used about my loving relationship with my wife. This went a long way toward healing my fear of homosexuals as I resonated with their celebration of their loving relationships.

Intent is the choice of which potential reality you will adopt. Intent is expressed in many ways. Every action, physical posture, emotional attitude, spoken word, internal dialogue, visualization, breath dynamic, sound expressed internally or externally and an infinite number other aspects of life express intent. Underlying all intent is belief. When you embrace opposing beliefs you create disease. This disease may manifest on any level including physical, intellectual, emotional and spiritual.

This is an example of a family I worked with as a co-therapist with Chardin Bersto, M.A., and illustrates this interplay of belief and intent and how it affects health. A long time client called me and insisted that I must see his wife immediately. She had just undergone a double mastectomy as the result of breast cancer. She was told that her chances of survival for six weeks was about 35 percent. She came to she us to appease her husband's demands. It was immediately apparent that she was the *heart of the family*. The family included a teen age son, a married daughter in her early twenties, the daughter's husband and an infant child. The woman was very clear in the belief that she was dying because her family was falling apart.

We decided that the whole family must be involved in the healing process. The children put up heavy resistance at first. Her husband had been extremely domineering and was described as a tyrant. He agreed that this had been the case in the past, but assured us that he was willing to change in order to help his wife survive. The family members were suspicious of me and my co-therapist but agreed to at least try what we suggested to help their mother choose to live. She had stated clearly that she intended to die if her family could not come together and act like a family.

After bringing the family together in my office, the mother began to make some progress in healing. She responded to the stated intent of the family to begin to work out their differences. The turning point in her healing process came a few weeks later. Her husband almost dragged her into my office. She had decided that her family wasn't sincere in the efforts to become a functional family. She stated that she wasn't going to do anything to survive. She was committed to dying.

She sat defiantly, daring us to try to talk her out of dying as soon as possible. She and her husband were both shocked when we refused to try to change her mind. We assured her that if she chose death, we would support her fully. I began to work with her to prepare herself to die in a loving way, leaving no unfinished business behind. Chardin worked with her sobbing husband to help him accept, that if she chose death, there was nothing anyone could do but support her in her resolve. We assured them that death is the appropriate end to life. When you die, it should be with the loving support of your friends and family—anything less would be selfish. The result of this session was that she chose life. Her husband chose to honestly work with her and the children to create a healthy family. The children were still suspicious, but were willing to find and work with their own therapists after their father admitted to the many crimes he had committed against them and their mother. The family confessed its deepest secrets. They claimed responsibility as the offenders and the healing process began in earnest for the mother, each family member and the family as a unit. As the family healed, so did the mother, despite her refusal to give up smoking and drinking. Six months later, her oncologist informed her that she was in remission. A year and a half later, when I last saw her, she was very healthy and still in complete remission.

Her family was healing as she hoped. All violence stopped after the children found that they could confront their parents with the offenses that were committed against them in the past without fear of retaliation. The children were willing to truly cooperate after they found that no matter how far or how hard they pushed their father, he would no longer strike out at them or act in a tyrannical manner. Each family member gained self-respect and self-esteem. They had reason to survive as a family and their mother had reason to survive as a person.

The husband's intent in this example is equally important in his wife's healing process. He admitted to being manipulative and demanding control over the family. This reflected his belief that he had the right and duty to be in control of his family. Not being in control meant that he was a failure as a man, a father and a husband. He believed he had the right to use violence to maintain his dominance.

A country western ballad called *Daddy* constantly went through his mind. This ballad was about a man who died and was seen as tough but fair by his surviving children. During his lifetime he was seen as a tyrant. This song constantly reaffirmed his beliefs about the nature of being a man and fueled his intent to continue his strategy toward his family. Although, he promised to change, his real intent was to continue his tyranny. He believed he would be able to force his wife and children to live up to his expectations until his wife made him realize that he was not in control. In fact, he never had been in control.

When she demonstrated to him that she could die without his consent, his world was upset. The inconsistency in his beliefs and what was happening in the world caused panic attacks that required hospitalization. During the family healing process, he felt helpless at first. His panic attacks revealed his intent that someone fix his life for him. Underlying this intent was the belief that he was unable to do anything to affect his own healing, but someone else could do it for him. It also revealed the belief that he was right all along and had no reason to try to change. His healing began when he admitted to himself and his family that he had never intended to change before. Now that the stakes were his wife's life, he finally gave in and worked to change in earnest. This willingness to change removed one more barrier to his wife's healing process.

His promise to change was echoed many times in his past. His children came to distrust everything he said and did. Although, he believed that his treatment of his family was for their own good, the family knew it wasn't in their best interest. Even after his wife began to believe that he was actually willing to change, the children remained unconvinced.

The children refused to consider changing their behaviors and attitudes until they felt safe in the knowledge that their father was finally sincere. They confronted him with his past crimes against them one after another. When he listened and accepted his responsibility they began to believe that he might be trusted.

Being his children, they believed that they had the right to punish him for his crimes. It was what he taught them by his actions. They began to escalate mirroring his violent and unreasonable behavior that they had been the target of throughout their lives.

When they were satisfied that he believed he had been

wrong in his treatment of them, they began to change their intent toward the family in general. The belief that the family was worth saving began to grow. Their father demonstrated his change of heart by refusing to retaliate, no matter how outrageously they behaved toward him. He had to admit that they were doing what he taught them. He realized that the only way to teach them another, more loving way was to demonstrate it by his behavior.

At the turning point in her healing process, her intent was to punish her husband because of his insincerity. He convinced her and the children that he was willing to change. They felt betrayed when he didn't change. He gave lip service to changing, but his actions stated that he was not willing to take responsibility for himself and his past.

She stubbornly chose death. It was her choice and if it wasn't honored, she felt that she wasn't honored. Her upbringing dictated that she must honor her husband and the only way out of the marriage was death. Her intent was to leave the marriage. Her belief was that the only way out of her suffering was death. She intended to die.

As I helped her prepare for her death, she began to see that she had many reasons to live. She chose to change her belief that she was a failure as a person, mother and wife. With this change of belief came a change in intent. She now intended to live. Her smoking and drinking, however revealed her belief that she may change her mind. She still retained the option to choose death if she had been tricked again into believing that her family was willing to change. Her intent to heal was greater than her intent to die.

If you respect yourself totally, you have no source of disrespect to project onto the world outside. Your intent toward others is also your true intent toward yourself. If a person has a stressful lifestyle, he or she will cause a buildup of substances in his or her body that may result in cancer or heart disease. The constant supply of stress hormones may contribute to ulcers, arthritis or diabetes. The inability to accept or give unconditional love may result in depression or drug abuse. The need to be right may result in psychological, emotional, physical and spiritual abuse.

Spiritual

There is an aspect of existence that interacts with the body and gives it life. Without this aspect, the body becomes a corpse. In practice, this aspect appears to transcend the life of the body in that some people easily experience prenatal states of existence. Others experience what they interpret as past lives.

Kirlian photography reveals some interesting findings about the energetic bodies that appear to infuse everything. When we cut a limb from a plant Kirlian photography shows that from an energy field standpoint, the limb still exists and before a new leaf grows, the energy outline exists. The material part of the newly forming leaf conforms to and fills the preexisting energy outline. Physical or emotional wounds appear in the energy field of a person in a similar way. These wounds often correspond to present life trauma, but sometimes they do not.

Sometimes during closed-eye or altered-states therapy such as hypnosis, people will experience what is commonly thought to be past life trauma as a contributing factor to their current difficulties in life. John, a man with a lifelong explosive temper, found his chronic anger was due to a previous life experience of dying on a battlefield. John was duped into going to war in the name of God and felt ultimately betrayed as he froze to death in an ice encrusted mud puddle as men rushed by and over him. As he lay there dying, he created so much anger and hatred toward God that he went through a succession of lives as a soldier that lasted for several thousand years. The experience during altered- state therapy helped him release the intense hatred and find a deeper peace which had eluded him all his life.

Gale, a woman with chronic throat problems, experienced being beheaded in ancient Greece. She sensed dying of throat cancer in other lives. During the present and past lives, Gale was finding no resolution to her throat problems. I suggested she go to a time and place where she could heal this succession of past life throat conditions. Gale experienced what she believed to be a future life where she was healed by a device that emitted sound and light. Gale's throat problem improved after these visions.

Relating to life challenges from the belief in past life trauma allowed healing to happen for these people. Regardless of the validity of reincarnation, working heartfully within that system of belief can bring about profound healing in some cases. Rather than reincarnation, another explanation might be memory or energy-field traces that exist in the atmosphere surrounding the earth. Each of us may be influenced by parts of memory traces from many past lives. If past life work is appropriate, the experience will present itself by being present with the communication from your life challenge. Whatever presents itself, allow your relationship with it to be whatever it is. Just meet your life challenge heartfully and without judgment on any level or through any sensory means that presents itself.

Robert O. Becker, M.D., an orthopedic surgeon and medical researcher refers to the current of injury (CI) as a measurable, low voltage, direct current flow of energy that streams from the injured area. In an article appearing in the 1991 issue of *The International Society for the Study of Subtle Energy and Energetic Medicine* (*Subtle Energies*),

Dr. Becker reports his research into what I have been calling the *soft body*. I derived the term soft body from Stephen Levine's work. This energetic aspect of all living things is also known as the light body, the energy body, the soul, the holy ghost, ki, chi and shakti. Whatever you call it, an energy field inhabits our bodies and when it leaves, our bodies become corpses.

Dr. Becker found a constant field of low voltage, direct current in living beings that interacts with the nervous system. This is possibly the force that caused the original development and evolution of the nervous system. His research supports the idea of an energetic outline existing for amputated limbs that acts as a mold for newly forming tissue. He found that if you cut off a salamander's leg (a salamander can grow a new leg), that an energetic outline of the leg exists with a negative, direct current flow. This means the energy flowed from outside the salamander's body into its wound. In a frog (a frog cannot grow a new leg), the same thing happened except the direct current was positive and flowed outward instead of inward. He also found the more awareness given to the wound, the greater the direct current flow to the injury or energetic outline. He proved this by measuring the CI of the salamander under anesthesia and as it became alert again. Researchers found that reversing the direction of current in the salamander's brain made it unconscious. When they reversed the current flow in an anesthetized salamander, it regained consciousness although the drug was still in the salamander's brain. The degree of consciousness of the salamander was measured by the intensity of the charge of the DC electrical field in it's brain. The degree of consciousness or awareness in the wound was measured by the intensity of the flow of electricity in the CI or current of injury. Thus, the more direct current (awareness) that existed in the area of the wound, the faster the injury healed.

This highlights the need for pain as part of the healing process. Of course, if the pain is severe you probably won't listen to it or have any desire to cooperate with it.

Dr. Becker found, in working with people, there are many ways to control the flow of energy in this energetic body, but none worked better than hypnosis. The potential to control the energetic body is our choice. *Energy follows awareness.* This is the basis of true energy work. It is a system of working consciously and directly with the soft body.

Dr. Becker's research shows the cells, at the end of each nerve ending and neural connection to the spinal cord called Schwann cells, act as communication relays for the soft body. Acupuncture points are usually at these relay stations. Meridians connect these acupuncture points throughout the body. This direct current outline of the soft body may create the energetic outline for the developing physical body. Dr. Becker thinks the direct current field of the energetic body promotes healing from the relay stations. He speculates this energetic body could reach out and touch others and gain knowledge about others through this touch as experienced in the grounding exercise.

Bring any attitude into your awareness. You might choose one that has caused you problems in the past. Perhaps you get angry at your spouse in a certain situation or you feel fearful in different situations. Feel that attitude inside. Notice what happens to your body, your thoughts and your feelings. Allow a person to come to mind. This person will be the appropriate person. It may be someone you met only once thirty years ago or a movie star. You have adopted the attitude in question as a result of making a contract with this person to join with them in this attitude.

Notice where on your body this joining is. You may find that the attitude is attached to your heart or your toes or any other place, even some that don't seem to be inside your body. It is more important to notice where the attitude attaches to your body than who the original contract was with. If you recognize who is involved in this contract you may choose to release them by name and seal the place of attachment by putting your hand on it and intending that it seal. Each of these connections or contracts are a source of draining your energy and a coloring of your overall life. Many people may be attached to you in this manner and influence all aspects of your life through these attachments. When a person dies these attachments may cause problems for both the deceased and the living.

We can experience how our life energy attaches to various objects, people and ideas. When we infuse an idea with some of our life energy, it becomes a living being in a way similar to the way our bodies become alive when this spirit infuses them. We can attach bits of our life energy to many people, places and ideas while we are still living. Shamans call this loss of soul and it is the basis for Shamanistic healing. In our daily lives we infuse many ideas, events, relationships and material objects with our life energy. In the Shaman's view, each bit of attached energy takes away from the energy we have available for living or healing. By attaching some of our energy, we open ourselves to the influence of these energy bubbles. They become like living beings that survive by consuming our energy and the energy of others who attach to them. It's like coming into contact with the carrier of an infectious disease while decreasing the energy you have to counteract the infectious agent. Each of these attachments becomes a constant drain of energy and a source of stress until you release the attachment and withdraw the flow of energy.

While you imagine the images offered in the next paragraphs, I invite you to notice the way in which you experience them. Many people, myself included, do not actually see the images as in a dream. Visual images are only one type of imagery. Notice what you do when you pretend or daydream. You may not see an actual image in your mind. You may have a fleeting thought, voice or feeling. It makes no difference what form of imagery you use since you automatically use the form best for you at the moment. The form may change from minute to minute, but you will always find what you need if you are willing to accept it in the form offered. What you do with it after that is up to you. The imagery you use in meditations and in guided imagery will probably match those images you use in daydreaming, planning or remembering.

Imagine being born in deep space. You have a protective bubble that surrounds you and protects you. As you are born, you have one thin connection to that which exists outside your bubble—your mother. This connection is like an invisible tube that has awareness flowing back and forth through it between you and your mother. You give some of your energy to her, and she gives energy to you.

At some point, another person, usually a doctor or midwife touches you, and you connect with a smaller tube to the new person. Awareness flows back and forth. Now a bubble exists between your mother and the second person. You connect with this bubble and find no living being in it. Instead, there are emotions, personal history and beliefs infused with life energy from your mother and the second person. You will, as a matter of human nature, add a little of your life energy to the bubble and accept the boundaries defined by the beliefs in this bubble.

A third person touches you in some way. You reach out, in innocent curiosity, and connect with this person and the existing bubble between this third person, the second person, your mother and each of the others. For each person who touches you, the number of connections to idea bubbles grows at an accelerating rate. Each of these connections takes a little of your personal life energy.

In the philosophy of Ayurveda all energy has consciousness and all things have energy, so all things have consciousness. Saying that energy follows thought or awareness is a different way of saying that energy is consciousness.

Deepak Chopra in his book *Quantum Healing* reports on the case of a man who died and returned to life. When asked what he had experienced on the other side of the light, he said, "I experienced that I was conscious." When asked what he was conscious of, he replied, "I was conscious that I was conscious."

In the spiritual realm all techniques cause changes on all levels. If you intend for something to happen, and you have no opposing beliefs, emotional charges or physical stances, you will cause the thing you intend. Again, the intent brings the awareness of the proper action to cause a goal to become fact in the real world. If you follow the guidance and take this action, you will probably reach your intended goal. If you consistently ignore this guidance and action, you probably won't reach your goal.

Intent follows awareness which follows intent. Or as the therapeutic touch practitioners say, energy always follows awareness, or energy follows thought, or more simply they say, *life energy is awareness*. The exercises throughout the book will help you find ways to use life energy in your daily life.

Emotional

Stanislov Grof, M.D., assigned all experiences to coexes or compressed systems of experience. Each coex contains sensory, biographical, perinatal and transpersonal experiences that are related and have a common emotional charge. These systems or bubbles of experience are held together by the common emotional charge in the same way as matter is held together by a charge of sound. Grof uses sound and breath to access these coexes.

Emotions are powerful forces in our lives. They can overcome the best reasoning and understanding of any situation and leave us looking like fools. The wiring for emotions exists in our brains long before the circuitry for intellect develops. All circuitry for speech and visual processing passes through the emotional part of the brain. The neural impulses passing through these circuits are subject to emotional clearance and censoring before they go to the thinking area of the brain. The emotional part of the brain may hold the circuitry to all but the basic life support functions hostage, by blocking the passage of neural impulses. From the influence of emotions, everyone experiences impaired judgment. Anger, fear, guilt and jealousy are among the most common and sometimes occur when you embrace conflicting beliefs. It's an unhappy position to be in when you are against yourself. Your immune system, in essence, feels the same emotions as the larger you feels. Any emotional impairment also impairs your immune system. Bringing emotion into awareness, with the intent of changing it to a healthier emotion, promotes healing and the awareness of the actions needed for further healing. Like the sensations of your physical body, your emotions are an accurate map to your overall state of being.

Emotions play your body like a musical instrument and create a kinesthetic image within your body. As you focus on your emotions in a given situation, the ways in which they reach into the different facets of your life will begin to become more apparent. Some people refer to this web of emotion that resonates within as the emotional body. The beliefs and choices associated with your emotions become clearer as you become more aware of your emotional body.

Intellectual

The intellectual realm is our belief system. Beliefs are internal images of our world as we have come to expect it to behave. We have many beliefs of which we aren't aware, but all the same these beliefs operate in our lives. All beliefs are the result of the way we relate to the world—self-talk, body posture, emotional stance, musculature, attitude, motion, etc. These aspects reflect your beliefs about reality.

You change your beliefs through awareness. When you bring a belief into awareness, you update the belief along with the other beliefs you hold according to your current intent in life. You release a belief when there is no remaining belief structure to support it. At times, entire limiting belief structures collapse by releasing a single supporting belief. When you learned there was no Santa Claus, that single change caused the collapse of an entire set of beliefs that you had to give up. If there was no Santa, then there was no Rudolph, no Mrs. Claus, no elves and so on. You asked, "Where did all those presents come from?" You knew everyone older had been lying to you. What else had they been lying to you about? "Next thing they will tell me is the Easter Bunny is a lie, too."

We seem to have a safety feature that allows this collapse

to take place at a rate that prevents death and usually prevents a psychosis. Children seldom go into a deep depression when they realize their parents lied to them about Santa and the Easter Bunny. They may mourn the loss, but the betrayal will probably be buried in the mind. The betrayal may return later in another form or as a vague distrust of adults. As you get older, you gradually release the belief that you can't trust adults. But, you may find that you still don't trust certain people like teachers, principals, doctors, judges, preachers, police or others in positions of authority.

We embrace and release beliefs only according to our choice or intent to do so. We maintain beliefs by choice. Stress occurs when you hold opposing beliefs to those of your family, society or yourself. This may eventually develop to a more serious problem. Being against yourself is a hard position to be in.

Physical

Your body entails the seemingly solid aspects of your being. However, your body isn't solid. Even your bones, if viewed in time lapse photography, are in a constant state of flux. According to modern physics, the empty space in the human body, at an atomic level, is in proportion to the empty space in the universe. Your body is the slowest vibrating manifestation of your total being. It's the physical expression of all the aspects and relationships of your beliefs and personalities.

Your body is the most concrete part of your greater self and may provide many clues about the greater you. It is the most available and accurate guide to the action necessary for any desired healing.

Chapter 4
Life Energy

In this chapter, we will explore life energy in a variety of ways. We tend to misunderstand the nature of a human being. We try to define the dynamics of the human system according to what we can observe, but the total human seems to defy our understanding. The physical, emotional and intellectual aspects of being human have been defined, but the subtle energy realm isn't as well known. More complex electronic devices are always being invented to measure and analyze the energetic nature of life. There are new highly sophisticated electroencephalographs (EEGs) that measure the brain waves, magnetic resonance imagers (MRIs), CAT and PET scanners and more. Research shows we interact with other energy systems, as well. Experiments detect that the electromagnetic field around plants and even rocks changes as we approach them. Plants react with what we might call fear if we intend to cut off their stems or leaves. The same plants relax when we approach to water them. The exercises throughout this book give you a feel for how this awareness works.

The body of universal energy (life energy) operates in a way that is similar to the universal water body that permeates all things within the earth's atmosphere except that it is not confined to the earth.

Life energy is an aspect of human nature that is important in any healing process. The movement of our life energy is a reflection of our total intent in life. The works of Milton Erickson are full of references to using preexisting resource states. Here, you go back to find something that you did, in the past, which could help you in your present situation. Perhaps you have to give a speech and you are terrified of speaking to groups, but as a young man you were in a band and had no problem playing before crowds. You may use these positive resource states to help in the present situation. By doing so you recreate the energy patterns that you used at an earlier time. All forms of energy work presume that energy follows thought or awareness and is directed by intent. By becoming aware of a past situation, you automatically cause your energy field to mimic the energy patterns you used then.

Earlier, we discussed the way a plant projects an energetic outline of a leaf before it begins to grow the physical leaf. This energetic outline acts as a mold which is filled by the emerging leaf. The energetic outline represents the intent of the plant. It is impossible to say for certain where the intent originates or what form it may take in a plant.

In humans every thought, movement, emotion and attitude is an envelope for delivering intent. As with the plant, the intent creates a mold that will be filled by your life energy. All energy is consciousness that fills any available form in order to express itself and thereby experience. The life energy infuses this mold in a way similar to the way it infuses your body. In a sense what ever you create by providing the energetic mold for the expression of your life energy becomes an almost independent life form. Everyone has experienced emotions or ideas that seem to take on a life of their own.

As you become more aware of your energetic nature you will begin to notice what supplies the intent that allows your life challenge to exist. The form that supports your life challenge may have facets that include heredity, social conditioning, family dynamics, beliefs, emotions, spiritual relationships and physical attitudes. There are certainly other possible sources for creating the energetic mold of your life challenge. You can discover these aspects yourself as the result of knowing yourself with honesty and clarity.

Chapter 5

Working with the Physical Body

Your physical body is a quick and accurate guide to your emotions and beliefs. Your body carries memories of the insults, physical and mental, that have been inflicted upon it in the past. A person physically assaulted as a child will usually turn their face quickly away from an approaching hand even if the hand is moving very slowly and the person's eyes are closed. Any physical wounds may have disappeared. Yet the wound still exists as an emotional charge in the body.

The beliefs of a person reflect in her or his body posture and attitude. A defiant person pushes his chin forward restricting his breathing. To check this out, take a deep breath and notice how deeply you inhale. Now, push your chin forward one inch and notice what happens to your breathing. This chronic breathing problem, by itself, has long-term health results. When you add restricted blood flow from tight shoulder and neck muscles and the frequent anger-kicks of adrenaline and neurotransmitters into the blood stream, it's easy to see how prolonged defiance is harmful to your health.

These beliefs probably produce poor eating habits and abuse of substances such as food, alcohol, tobacco, caffeine and other drugs. Your attitudes directly affect your health.

Several signposts reveal your true intent toward life—soft body dynamics, emotions, basic beliefs, body attitudes and stances, patterns of breathing and movements. Each signpost has a physical part that may be revealed by bringing your awareness to your physical body.

Grounding is the first step in working with the physical body. Always take a moment to bring your awareness into your body and release all thoughts about anything that has happened or may happen in your life. You must bring your awareness into the present. The next step is to probe your body with your awareness and locate a place of pain, tension or distress.

Now that you have found the physical location of the pain or discomfort, bring your awareness to it with the intent that it heals. You begin to release any emotion or belief related to the pain. Bathing the pain in your awareness and intent to heal is the most direct and powerful technique. Still, many people need to translate the intent and pain into symbols. Words, visual images, feelings, sounds, movement patterns and colors are sensory symbols that may be used to express intent.

Levels of the Brain

The human brain is made up of several layers. In essence, there are three brains starting with the brain stem (reptilian). The brain stem controls your heart and lungs. If we had to control these functions consciously, we wouldn't live long.

This lower layer also directs the flight or fight response. It mainly produces alpha waves corresponding to quiet awareness or mindfulness. It's like a frog sitting on a riverbank. The frog is aware of any movement or change around it. He is unaware of creatures or things that stay the same or move very slow. His only interest is with the quick changes happening around him. He just waits for food to come along. If there is movement nearby, he either zaps the moving object if it is food, or flees if he is threatened. If there is no immediate danger, the reptilian brain doesn't interfere. All other signals pass through to a higher level. If there is an immediate need or danger, the reptilian complex can override messages to a higher brain. Instead, it channels all available energy to flight or fight responses. All higher brain functions depend on the reptilian brain in that all neural wiring passes through it on the way to the next layer which is the old mammalian brain.

The next layer, the old mammal brain, is the place of emotions. (A dog has a reptilian brain with a more advanced brain on top of it. A dog can feel the full range of emotions that a human feels.) In humans all neural input is routed through the old mammal brain. The messages are subject to clearance by the emotions before they can move into the next higher complex. The emotional brain uses a strategy of matching. It sees how things are the same as opposed to the reptilian strategy of dealing only with differences. If the lower reptilian brain doesn't see an event as a matter of survival and the old mammal layer has no high emotional charge, the unrestricted input passes through to the brain where reasoning takes place.

The new mammal brain is similar to the brain found in apes. This layer can ponder the emotions of the old mammal brain. The ape suffers, seeks pleasure and has some form of self-talk. The ape can form basic beliefs. If an event isn't a matter of survival, an affair of the emotions, or a basic belief, the signals pass through to the newest developing brain, the frontal lobe. Dr. Dee Coulter calls this the *angel* brain.

In humans, the frontal lobe is the seat of altruism. Great

apes, humans, whales and dolphins have frontal lobes. Experts believe it doesn't process language but is the place that processes the highest human functions such as love and compassion. Having only our human brains to think with, we'll likely never be able to fully comprehend the entire human brain. Building a total brain capable of working with ever more subtle and difficult concepts is similar to how computer development works, leaving evolution of the brain always in the lead. By the time software is developed to use the capabilities of a new computer, that computer is fast becoming obsolete.

All pain impulses must rise and clear through each of the layers of the brain. If there is pain and the reptilian layer can't deal with it by fight or flight, the brain stem may allow pain signals to move to the next layer. If the old mammal brain can't deal with it by emotional charges, it may allow the pain signals up to the new mammal complex. Here it is reasoned out or passed on to the frontal brain where high-level processing occurs in a way that we don't yet understand. For this whole process to occur in the physical body, each level must let go and allow the pain signals to rise to a higher layer. The process of moving to more developed layers may be frustrated by any of the lower brains' failure to allow parts more suited to the task to take control.

In the soft body with its framework of relay stations and energy fields throughout, the roadblocks of ego, belief and emotion may be bypassed. Considering the layers and functions of the brain, we can begin to see how emotional pain might reflect in the body. Pain sent to the frontal lobes would have a counterpart in all three lower layers.

Yoganidra

Our society doesn't teach us to experience our bodily

sensations. The following is a yoga exercise called Yoganidra. This exercise will help you become more aware of what is happening inside your body. It also is a means of quick relief from stress. You may want to have another person call out the body parts for you as you do this exercise. It is helpful then to switch roles—where you name the body parts while your partner does the exercise.

Close your eyes. Have someone name a part of your body. You respond by bringing your awareness to that part. You may want to use some internal signal to acknowledge the contact. Imagine hearing a bell ringing in the body part or seeing it in your mind's eye light up. Have another body part named and touch it with your awareness. Have your partner continue naming parts of your body, calling out the parts faster and naming smaller parts until you can no longer keep up. If you are alone, you can silently name the parts while following them in your mind.

Another variation of this exercise is to move back and forth between places in your body where you experience opposite feelings. For example, you may move from: tension to relaxation, pain to pleasure, anxiety to ease, depression to excitement or boredom to adventure.

Your body is the most available screen to project your beliefs onto. Any belief, with its emotional charge or attitude, can be experienced in more ways inside yourself than in the outside world. If, for example, you believe that all dogs are vicious as a result of once being bitten by a dog, you will find memories to reinforce this view. You will have your own and other's stories, pictures and movies about vicious dogs. You may possibly find only one personal experience of a dog bite, yet, you have an amazing sequence of vicious dog thoughts. Perhaps you are not even the one who was bitten, but you felt so much empathy for the bitten person that you have created this vicious dog reality with no personal experience. You have imagined this false reality.

As children we are led to believe many things that we will never experience. These are written within, but most of them aren't found in the outside world. Your world within must be larger than your outside world. Your world within is the template through which you experience the outside world. In the instance of the person with the vicious dog belief, it will be nearly impossible for him to experience a friendly dog. His distrust and preconceptions about dogs will cause dogs to distrust and fear him. His feelings will also cause him to actively avoid dogs. He will not be open to a setting where his belief can be changed.

We all too often get lost in the negative and unpleasant places in our bodies and forget there are as many positive and pleasant places. As you discover the amazing world inside your body, you find that it contains everything that exists outside. Similarly, you can't experience something you don't believe in with senses you don't know you have. All your sensory capabilities start from within your body as your body is the instrument of your sensory experience. Your ability to sense inside is the same as your ability to sense outside. The same is true of your ability to experience. If you haven't found it inside, you cannot find it outside. Your world inside must be larger than your world outside.

Your body is a perfect mirror of how you feel and what you believe at any given time. In this mirroring exercise you can experience this dramatically. Have a person stand in front of you. Begin to adjust your body so it matches their posture. Ask them any questions that you need to find out things, like where they are tense and how much of their weight is on each part of their feet. Have them guide you into their exact posture. As you get closer to matching their posture, notice what this posture makes you think about. How does it makes you feel? What is its attitude?

Have them think of a situation in which they felt strong emotion. Have them guide you in matching the shifts that they made in their body as they began to bring this memory into their awareness. See if you can guess the details of their memory. You will be surprised at the detail that is relayed through another person's body attitude and posture.

Personifying the Pain

Personifying the pain is a type of inner child work. I caution you against doing inner child work without the guidance of a professional therapist. This work may evoke traumatic memories and flashbacks. If you don't feel safe doing this work with a certain therapist, find one that you do feel good about.

Once you bring your awareness to the pain, gently probe the area. Notice the quality of the pain. Is it a burning, itching, tense or tearing pain? Feel what kind of pain it is. Find the epicenter or where the pain begins. Begin to trace the pathways of the pain. How far from the center of the pain does it reach. Notice the direction, length and shape of the pain. Notice its texture and weight. Is it hard or soft?

Be aware of the quality, shape, size, color and location of the pain. Then personify it on any level of expression. You might ask it to speak to you. Many people find this easy to do. You can talk to the pain. Inner conversation means you are working with beliefs. With beliefs, you are likely to spark emotions that can be softened or released.

Once you are fully aware of the pain, you can ask it to talk with you in your mind. If this is difficult, you might ask inside for a part of you to translate for the pain. Some questions that might be useful to ask of the pain are:

- Where did you start?
- What do want from or for me?
- What do you need?
- What do you allow me to do that I would not be able to do without you?

Be curious. Ask any questions you want. Remember to watch for limiting basic beliefs in the replies such as I am not worthy of living, I deserve pain or disease, I am bad or I have no control.

You can change these beliefs by choosing to change them. For example, if you ask a backache what it does for you, you might hear a voice inside your mind reply, "I protect you from people taking advantage of your giving nature." There are some beliefs that are clear here:

- You are a giving person.
- You can't say no, so you need an excuse to say no.
- You need protection from yourself and other people.
- People take advantage of you.

This reply gives you several avenues into the belief structure that supports the pain, discomfort or disease. Each limiting belief you change or release helps your overall environment change in a way that contributes to a healthier you. Inner child work is an effective way to work with emotional and belief content.

There are many forms of inner child work or reparenting techniques and any will work here. Remember that this inner child is you and you must now takeover as the parent in this child's life. You must treat this child as she needs to be treated (with respect) and not in the way your mother, father, siblings, teachers, clergy or others treated you.

Treat this inner child as a younger you who has been hurt and made to feel unacceptable. This child needs to know that he or she is welcome and lovable. If you find that you cannot accept the child, don't try to force it. It is possible that you are not ready to handle what would emerge. The guardian aspect of your ego protects you from recognizing anything that you can't cope with. Respect your own pace.

When you check inside you may hear something like, "It's like part of me always wants this and another part always wants the opposite." If your inner child has conflicting feelings, the following exercise may be useful.

Imagine that one of the opposing parts is in the palm of one hand and the other part is in the palm of the other hand. You may be interested in the choice of hands you put each image in. Some people think of the left as the feminine or the past and the right as masculine or the future. Ask your inner child what it means to him or her, if anything. Describe each image in detail and name them if you want. Ask each side to tell its story. After each side clearly presents itself, have the images turn and face each other and start talking to each other. As the talking progresses, the hands may begin to move closer together. If not, coax them very gently. The object is to get the two images to merge and then place the combined image into your heart. You may want to put the parts in bubbles that merge. Then merge the combined bubble with your heart, or use any other image that works for you.

One goal of inner child work is self-acceptance of the parts that you have rejected in the past. This causes an effect that is retroactive to the age at which the original trauma occurred. This self rejection can be the source of many conflicting beliefs and secrets.

Fritz Perls believed in the power of awareness. If you allow unhindered exploration of any issue, a healthier relationship with it occurs. Always respect all the parts of yourself as if they were separate people. Treat yourself with the same degree of respect you feel would be due to another person. In any situation you may always choose your attitude. When personifying a life challenge you may represent it as an animal, an adult, a child, a part of your higher self, a guide, a mystical being or any other symbol that works for you. Always be very flexible with symbols and their interpretation. The only interpretation that is important is your own. Ask inside to find out the meaning of anything that appears.

Pain sometimes is a sign of healing, change or growth. When you make dramatic changes in your life, you may become afraid and upset. With healing on any level, body pain, fever and nausea are common. You must rely on your senses and self-honesty to distinguish between symptoms of healing and symptoms of sickness.

Chapter 6
Beliefs and Emotions

Beliefs and emotions are presented together, because in real life they are inseparable. You can't tell whether beliefs precede emotions or vice versa. When working with the physical body, beliefs and emotions emerge.

Working with the belief system is examining beliefs and changing those beliefs that do not serve you. Often, you can change your beliefs by choice as long as the new belief fits into your general belief system. For example, if a person is afraid of bodies of water, he may change this belief by learning to swim. The fear of drowning usually comes from childhood warnings not to go too close to water. Even if it is only on a controlled and unconscious level, this person feels fear at the mention of a body of water. If the person learns to swim, the belief and the fear may change, along with his relationship with water.

According to Milton Erickson this is a process of reframing, or changing the meaning of an event. There are two forms of reframing: content and context. One example of context and content reframing comes from Erickson's work with a young girl with a wart on her hand. The wart had resisted all treatment. He found that the girl's grandfather, who had recently died, had accidentally brushed the back of her hand with his cigar on the spot where the wart formed. Erickson told the girl that the wart was a gift from her grandfather. This is content reframing: changing the wart from a large problem involving dragging the child to doctors to a gift or something to cherish. The meaning of the wart changed. Erickson also told the girl she should keep this precious gift until she finished grieving for her grandfather. It was her grandfather's way of staying with her a little longer. Erickson explained that her grandfather wanted her to let go of him gradually now that he was gone. The wart disappeared after several weeks. This example of context reframing or redefining changed the child's relationship with the wart.

Working with beliefs can be powerful, but if the belief system isn't consistent with the emotional, energetic or physical belief, change won't occur on a deep level. If the child's family had been poor and she was shamed and hit because she had a wart requiring medical care that the family could not afford, changing only the intellectual belief would be of little use. The physical body belief would be that she was in physical danger. The emotional change might be guilt or shame for having needs requiring help that was not financially available. The energetic or spiritual belief might be that she does not belong or is not welcome in this life and that she deserves to have warts because she isn't pretty.

Working with the emotional system is a process of accessing and changing the supporting beliefs. Also, it is contacting and releasing the related emotional charges and physical attitudes. Beliefs that limit or restrict a person must change to promote deep healing. A single limiting belief can hold a person hostage. One belief can prevent change or cause a person to behave in ways that are harmful. Beliefs, at times, just fade away to be replaced by updated beliefs. Or, a person may cling to a belief against overwhelming evidence. The same is true of emotional charges and physical attitude.

It is often revealing to state what you believe about your life challenge. The results are usually surprising. Take a pencil and paper and begin to write about your life challenge. Write quickly without worrying about style, grammar or making sense. Write for twenty minutes without stopping. Just write whatever comes into your mind. You are free to throw this paper away without showing it to anyone. After you have finished, write for another fifteen minutes as if you were your life challenge.

When you are in touch with a life challenge, you can usually state the beliefs associated with it. Common beliefs that might surface are, "I am no good; I deserve punishment; I am not lovable; I am not worthy; I don't belong or I am not welcome." You can recognize these beliefs in your life if you listen for them. Notice that each of these phrases causes an emotional response when you say them to yourself. Repeat them several times and notice the way your posture and feelings change as you read each.

You can often change beliefs by simply stating them and deciding to change them. You can usually release emotional charges and muscular attitudes by repeatedly experiencing them with the intent that they change. Again, this is a process of awareness and intent.

Self-Talk

The power of internal self-talk is well-known. Within our realities nothing that exists is without a supporting belief. Thus, we experience only that which we believe. If you don't believe something exists, you cannot perceive it. A belief is a part of the template that we use to experience our worlds. All experience is compared to our personal templates. Everyone experiences a setting differently. At crime scenes, police often get a different story and description of the suspects from each witness. Each witness adapts the experience to fit into his or her own belief system. What they then see is a second-hand explanation of what happened given through their self-talk beliefs even though they witnessed the event first-hand. It's possible to experience first-hand without the filters of belief, but we rarely do that. Being present to act in the world instead of reacting to your self-talk is the only way to step outside the prison bars of your beliefs. Internal chatter clouds our accurate perception of the events.

Learning, conditioning and understanding create our self-talk beliefs. Our words become the boundaries of our experience or beliefs. For example, if our self-talk revolves around being a victim without control over our lives, we are anxious and feel lost much of the time. We know other choices exist, but we selectively experience life within the boundaries of our belief systems. If we live within the victim bubble, the beliefs available within this framework will support the illusion of being a victim.

As victims, we see only the filled parking spaces and not the empty ones. Or, if we do see the empty spaces, we may whine to ourselves that if we park in these spaces, someone may break into our car or steal it. If we believe that people will take advantage of us, we may walk past the people who will treat us with respect—as if they didn't exist. We may seek those who are looking for a victim. We imprison ourselves within the boundaries of the beliefs we choose.

These beliefs support and define our emotions and attitudes. When we act within the confinement of our belief systems, we are unable to be present in the moment. We trap ourselves in thinking about the past or rehearsing the future. Often, we react in the moment according to our beliefs, attitudes and emotional charges leaving us blind to the proper action here and now. In this way we limit our personal power.

The Secret

The role of the secret is a powerful force. You adjust your life to protect your secrets. Even if it's that little savings fund you've hidden from your spouse, a secret causes stress in your life. If your secret is that your parents are raging alcoholics and you are under constant threat of someone finding out, the stress increases. James Pennebaker, Ph.D., Professor of Psychology at Southern Methodist University, talks about how suspects often thank lie detector operators for helping them to confess. They experience a profound relief when they no longer have to bear their deepest criminal secrets.

The family secrets can often be deadly. I worked with a woman who had undergone a double mastectomy. Her doctors gave her only a short time to live. When I first saw her, she made it clear that this cancer was not about her, it was about her family. The way they treated each other was killing her and she would die if the family battles didn't stop. She stated her conditions for living, "I am going to die if these guys don't start learning how to get along. They don't have to be perfect. They just have to try to really care." My co-therapist and I worked with her and her family. As the family confessed their secrets, she began to change. Honest talk started again between family members. As her family moved toward better health, she also became more relaxed and healthier. The last I heard she was healthy and cancer free. Although her family was still having problems, they were making progress.

A popular technique to overpower negative beliefs is to

use positive affirmations. You begin by countering a negative thought or emotion with a positive thought. For example, we may say, "I never get what I want," which we may counter with, "I always get what I want." This simply creates another boundary and limits our awareness and options in the world. Always getting what we want is as limiting and maybe more potentially dangerous to us than never getting what we want. Often our conscious minds are as immature as a child's. Imagine what would happen if you got every childish, selfish or insensitive wish. If we strive to become clear of the boundaries of our beliefs, we become in a heartfelt way more versatile and can serve not only us but all life.

Positive affirmations may be steps in this direction, but the next step is to learn to escape the prison of our beliefs, emotions and attitudes. This is easier than overpowering negativity with positivity. When we have a thought that doesn't serve us, like, "He's such a so-and-so!" we could make up an affirmation. We might say, "I now see the greater good in all persons," and repeat this to ourselves until we have overwhelmed the original thought. We set ourselves up to ignore the ways in which this person might harm us. We can simply say, "I choose to release that thought, belief, attitude or feeling and its roots," or "I choose not to accept this thought as mine." As people we tune into the thoughts of those around us and often these so-called negative thoughts belong to someone else. That is, until we accept them into our belief systems on an unconscious level.

Affirmations are a shifting of the boundaries of experience and possible action in life. Releasing boundaries also releases limitations. Another practical definition of release is forgiveness.

As you choose to release these thoughts, emotions, attitudes and beliefs, you may feel like something is leaving your body. This releasing is an energetic and electrochemical event. When you choose to release that which you have embraced on a superficial level in your life, it may feel like something is floating away from you. If you choose to release something leftover from childhood, it may feel as if something profound has been released from the depths of your body. You may shudder as you feel it migrating through your entire body on its way out. A feeling of relief and having a weight lifted may pervade your being. The sensation is different for every person.

You may also find it good to withdraw your life energy from whatever you have released and to seal the energetic pathway of this connection to shield yourself from future reconnection.

As you release more and more beliefs and attitudes you become quieter inside. Your awareness of yourself and the outside world becomes increasingly clear. As you become more sensitive to the experiences in your life, more resources become available to you. More choices become available, and it's easier to act in the world with presence. The more you take notice of these subtle sensory sensations, the more you make choices from the reality of here and now instead of the illusions of past and future. Your actions become less clouded by beliefs and emotions.

Whenever you release something, it's very important to replace it with something you want or want more of in your life. As Wind Woman says, "Nature hates a vacuum—if you empty your basket and don't refill it with what you choose, it will fill with even more of the same poobah you just emptied."

When you release a rude thought you may say, "I choose to replace this with self-respect." Or, if you release an angry, unreasonable attitude, you may choose to replace it with a peaceful reasonable attitude. Some useful replacements are: presence, patience, kindness, compassion, strength, prosperity, fun, loving humor, knowledge or anything else you find appealing.

Affirmations can be powerful expressions of intent. In the way we just mentioned, use affirmations to clarify that which you choose to move toward as opposed to creating limiting beliefs. Saying, "I choose to have more fun in my life," is an effective affirmation.

When you release something and choose something else to replace it, you are automatically using affirmations. It isn't necessary, however, to release something to use affirmations.

Key words are single words or phrases that bring into awareness the various sensory images of the intent. For example, if you are working on healing, you may choose the word healthy to bring into your awareness your complete sensory image of what being healthy means to you. It's most desirable to express clearly your intent on a preverbal level to avoid the limitations of language. The words you use to describe something flavor it with the beliefs that those words represent to you. You also spike it with unwanted energy.

We commonly associate consciousness or awareness with thought. It's as if we believe that if we cease thinking, we will cease to exist. Subvocal thinking is a necessary expression of consciousness. There are many other expressions of consciousness such as feeling, emoting, seeing, visualizing, imagining and art. All life is an expression of consciousness. Native Americans believe that all things have consciousness. This must be true if the religions that believe in the oneness of all things, that all is of God, are right. The real power of the techniques presented in this book have nothing to do with thought, they all have to do with awareness. As you read the exercises and ideas, allow yourself to experience them in every way you can. To rely on thinking is an inefficient way of operating in the world. When you use your nonverbal senses, you are more efficient at most things. There are, of course, times when verbal thought is the best tool, such as when doing statistics or preparing a meal from a recipe. One way to view thinking is as a computer program that translates each step and command into people language. Working nonverbally is like using the machine language that has no need to translate anything into people language to operate. When performing a task with a computer, the machine language or hardware programming is much faster and more efficient than Basic, a computer language that uses plain English.

We learn how to operate the hardware of the body long before we learn to talk. We have the capacity of functioning nonverbally much of the time and yet we choose to mainly limit ourselves to a verbal world.

For example, it's more powerful to see yourself in a new job where you can hear the sounds, see and smell the surroundings, than to tell yourself over and over, "I want a new job." When you imagine the new job with all the sensory detail you can muster, you are more likely to know and take the action needed to get the job instead of just repeating the affirmation. Of course, if you don't act you won't get the job regardless of whatever else you do. It's always easier to act in the world if you stop the self-talk and act when you have decided to act. If you take action to get what you want in the world yet tell yourself that you can't possibly succeed or someone will take it away from you, it is much harder to act. Even if you do succeed, the joy may not be there. This constant self-defeating chatter drains energy and vitality.

The best reason for releasing these limiting beliefs,

emotions or attitudes is that it usually serves your best interests to do so. Changes made for the benefit of others only serve to create more limits in your life. I am not suggesting that you treat people heartlessly. I only want you to understand when you give to or serve others, you are doing it for yourself, because who you are demands that you offer service to express yourself in the world. To the person receiving your gift, it feels as though you are doing something kind for them. But, if you believe you are doing this good deed for them, you have changed it from a gift to a one-sided contract. It's like saying, "I have done this for the universe and I deserve this much in return." It's a fool's contract, like painting a house at random and then demanding the owner pay for the work. This puts you in the position of being a victim of the universe. When you understand that the reward of serving is the act of self-fulfillment, you are in a position of partnership and support with the universe.

Chapter 7
Techniques

In the practice of psychoneuroimmunology (PNI), a variety of practical techniques are available. The Taoist Priests have compiled more than twelve hundred volumes of writings on qigong, an ancient system similar to PNI. The most effective techniques are those that are natural and easy to use. Use them to guide you to what works best in a given situation. Be creative in your use of PNI.

Belief

When working with any life challenge, it is helpful to discover your beliefs about it. The beliefs which you choose set the limits of what you can know about your life challenge. They also limit the action you can take in response to your life challenge. The beliefs you hold are like theatrical scenery that you superimposed on the world around you. You act in your personal drama according to these beliefs. If you believe it is impossible to change your life to a more healthful way, you won't find the resources necessary to react in a healthier way. It isn't that these resources don't exist, your lack of belief simply leaves you blind to them. When the oncologist says that your cancer isn't serious and is treatable, you hear the doctor saying, "You have cancer and you're going to die and there isn't any hope for you." The belief (thinking) and emotion associated with the cancer has to pass before reason and judgment are possible. When you are stuck at the belief and emotional level, you have constant fear and stress.

It's like being given a calculus problem and you only have basic arithmetic to work with. Still, you keep on trying to find the solution. Similarly, in daily life, you may invest your energy in endless thinking—"If I were any good I'd be more successful, but if I were successful I would make a lot of money and people with money are bad so I can't be successful, but if I were any good I'd be successful." Your beliefs take away the chance of getting what you believe you need in life. Which, of course, is just another belief.

An example of limited beliefs is the young circus elephant. A thin rope tied to one of its legs holds the immature elephant. As a baby, the elephant is incapable of breaking the rope or pulling the stake from the ground. As the elephant grows, it believes that the rope is unbreakable though it has enough strength to snap the rope with a single tug. An old belief holds the elephant captive.

We tend to hold ourselves captive by beliefs that have no basis in any reality other than our own. Yet, we can update our beliefs and release the damaging attitudes and emotional charges by simply examining the beliefs in light of new knowledge. We also can do tasks that we believe are impossible if we are unaware that we are doing them.

A Russian weight lifter broke a world record after his trainer told him the weight on the bar was lower than the world record weight. The Russian had lifted this lower weight many times before. He hoisted the world record weight though he had never lifted as much before and believed that it was not possible for him to do so.

Throughout history each generation does feats thought impossible by the previous generations. When the beliefs change enough to allow the impossible to become the possible, the actual feat often follows closely. The impossible becomes the ordinary.

Every PNI exercise you do reveals certain aspects of your beliefs. If you represented your life challenge as a bear and you as a wounded lamb, in the personifying-the-pain exercises from Chapter 5, the belief that you are powerless in the face of your life challenge becomes part of the image. You will be powerless to affect your life challenge in a healthful way until you redefine the relationship between it and you.

The simplest exercise for discovering beliefs is to make a list of your thoughts about your life challenge. The beliefs that emerge may be surprising. Each belief about your life challenge holds an innate intent and listing these beliefs on paper or verbally is revealing. You may want to list your beliefs such as:

- how my life challenge serves me
- how it hinders me
- what it teaches me
- how others feel about it
- how I feel about it
- what it means about me
- how it interferes with what I want in life
- what it would be like to live to be 100
- what do my family and friends believe about my life challenge
- how do people treat me differently than if I did not have my challenge
- the motto that my family and I live by is . . .
- how do I want life to be if it could be any way that I choose
- what do I intend to achieve in my life
- what role does my pain play in my life

- what does it give me permission to do or say
  that I wouldn't do or say without my life challenge

Verbal probes are an effective way to discover beliefs about your life challenge. Probes are phrases that are supportive and positive. A probe is an offering of emotional nourishment. You react to the probe according to your beliefs and emotional charges about the related issue.

A sample probe might be something like, "You are perfect the way you are." The reaction could be anything from a sigh of contentment to an outburst of anger and tears.

To deliver a probe, ask yourself (or the receiving person if you are working with another person) to go inside and become a silent reporter. A reporter does not make judgments or interfere in any way, he just records all that he observes. Ask yourself or the person to notice any reactions to the probe. Some reactions include words, images, feelings, realizations, or the relaxing or tensing of muscles. Close your eyes. When you (or your partner) are ready, slowly say the probe, then repeat the probe. Notice the reactions without judging them as you say the words.

Some probes you might find useful are:

- I am perfect just the way I am
- I am (lovable, acceptable, worthy)
- I don't need to do anything to be (lovable, acceptable, worthy)
- I may claim a treasure from my relationship with my life challenge
- it is okay to heal now
- it is okay not to heal until you are ready
- it is okay to keep your life challenge until you no longer need it

All probes should be supportive and free of judgment.
Body-Centered Psychotherapy, The Hakomi Method, by

Ron Kurtz has a more complete list of probes and information on the use of probes.

Drawing your life challenge can reveal unconscious beliefs. Draw a picture of yourself, your life challenge, the action you have taken to heal, and your immune functions as they interact with your life challenge. Draw a second picture of the people in your life and how they support you in your healing process. Use crayons of as many colors as you want.

These drawings reveal many beliefs, attitudes and emotional charges. Notice the color or lack of color in the drawing. If color is sparse, this may show a lack of enthusiasm in life. If the picture is full of color, this may suggest an excitement about life and a desire to live. Red may show emotion or conflict. Black may be grief or depression. White on white paper may represent a cover-up or denial. Yellow might be energy. Orange can suggest change. Purple may show spirituality or support. Blue, green and brown may be neutral. These representations are only guidelines. Consider the colors available as they may be inaccurate in specific drawings. If the only color available is black, it would be ridiculous to consider it a sign of depression.

The colored body of the pictured person may give clues to a problem. If the person in the drawing lacks eyes, he may be hiding his problem. If the drawing has no feet, this might show a feeling of being stuck or unable to move. The lack of hands may show a feeling of being powerless. A missing nose may show inability to take in nourishment or life force. Missing ears might represent an unwillingness to listen or learn. Drawing only a part of the body where there is ample paper for a full body, may show a feeling of something missing or the inability to take an active part in the healing process. What is missing in the drawing can be more important than what is drawn.

If your life challenge is shown in a form that is more powerful than you or the treatment, it suggests that your life challenge is in control. If the drawing shows the immune functions as stronger than the life challenge, control over the life challenge is suggested.

The drawing of the support system may reveal the outside resources available to the person. The barriers caused by beliefs about the intent of the social environment and emotional charges associated with other people' and relationships may be revealed.

Dreams

Dreams are an important and readily available means for gaining greater insight into your life challenges. There are many techniques for analyzing dreams, but the only accurate assessment is yours. To understand a particular dream, bring yourself to a state of deeper, inner awareness using any method you choose. Move closer and closer to the dream state. When you are ready bring the dream more into your awareness by making the details sharper and clearer, the sounds more vivid and the feelings more present. This is like turning up the volume, intensity and brightness of your internal dream tube.

Begin reviewing the dream from the first part remembered to the last part remembered. The details become clearer as you progress. Let your inner wisdom translate the dream as you run it through your awareness again. If some meaning isn't clear, describe each detail of the dream as if talking to a being from outer space who knows nothing of life on earth. How would you describe a dog, a pen or a picnic table to an alien who had no ideas about these items? Describe each detail in your dream, no matter how ordinary, as if trying to teach an alien being. Choose any area of your life and ask yourself how these details fit into what is happening in that part of your life. What do they mean? What action might you take based on your dreams? Ask your higher mind to let this impression be about something specific, like your life challenge. If you have questions about the effectiveness of a plan or treatment in dealing with your life challenge, you need to ask that the answer be relevant to the treatment.

Another way to use dreams in your healing is to program your dreaming. One way to do this is to use any technique presented in this book as you fall asleep at night. Use dreams to continue the work that you have been doing. You may find yourself aware to heal in your dreams as you direct your immune system and other related aspects of your life. You may find that you understand profound things about your healing and your life energy as you work in this realm on the edge of consciousness. This knowledge, at times, disappears with the first flash of wakefulness. But, with practice you can recall more vividly the details of your dreams.

The last time I got the flu, it was a viral strain that most people suffered with for more than a week. I spent about thirty of the next forty-eight hours in a partial lucid dream state. I used sound, light, color and imagery to direct my white blood cells to kill the virus. Imagery helped me wash the wastes from the dead virus out of my body. I massaged sore muscles with the fingers of my soft body. I applied a healing, soothing salve to my cramped, dehydrated muscles. I used my soft body hands to balance the flow of energy through my body. After the forty-eight hours I was well again.

Had I attended to the warning signs when my body first began to alert me of poor nutrition, I might have avoided the flu. My immune system was weakened. My nutrition was lousy; I was dehydrated from not drinking enough water or providing adequate minerals; I didn't exercise; I wasn't relaxing at home or on weekends. I was aware of my poor lifestyle, but I didn't take heed so my lack of self-respect had to express itself in a more drastic way. If I had continued to ignore these things, I believe that the intent behind the lack of self-respect would have resulted in a louder cry for help from within myself. This cry might have been anything, from a ten-day bout with the flu to pneumonia, that would cause me to stop and examine my intent toward my life and my self.

Keeping a journal on dreams, insights, imagery or thoughts can help you to understand the aspects of different life challenges and how they relate to each other and the world. Keeping a life challenge journal is highly recommended.

I put together a workbook for my clients to help them become aware of various aspects of their life challenges. Bill, a businessman, saw immediately the reason he sabotaged his efforts in business after he drew a picture of his ideal life. Bill was surprised at what he drew. When he wrote down what he wanted in life, it became clear that the things he had told himself were important weren't really that important. Having identified his real intent in life—to enjoy his family first and his business second—made Bill's real intent much easier to fulfill.

Imagery

Imagery is important in all PNI techniques. As a technical note, there is a difference between imagery and visualization: when you see a generic book in your mind's eye, that is a visualization; when the book becomes a specific book that you have feelings about and that has a story attached to it, that is imagery.

As you approach any life challenge with the intent to heal it, it is helpful to first form a representation of the life challenge to interact with it. We have explored personifying the life challenge, experiencing some energetic qualities it has and discovering the beliefs, emotional charges and physical attitudes that form around it. Each of these involves different forms of imagery. Each is an abstract representation of the same life challenge. Each makes a valid representation, in the language of its own form of imagination—much like the way we represent things when we talk.

Different languages use different sounds, rhythms and inflections to represent the same idea. All are valid within their language, but may make little sense in a different language. If you go into a Japanese restaurant, where only Japanese is spoken and understood, and you try to order a meal in Swedish the words won't make any sense to the waiter. Within each language is the framework to allow people to talk with each other.

This is equally true with the language of imagery. For example, if in your mind's eye you see everything threatening as large and looming, you can show a lack of threat by making the images small and distant. Or if you have a fever, you might lower your body temperature by imagining yourself in a snow bank. Imagery is the mind's way of showing our intent.

The automatic function of imagery theory states that by making an image, the unconscious mind begins to guide you toward the intended action or goal. Thus, you have delivered the intent in a form to which your unconscious mind responds. Your unconscious mind brings the necessary guidance and sensory feedback into your awareness to allow you to complete the intent.

A Safe Place

When using imagery, it is helpful to create a safe place or sanctuary. If you don't feel safe, you can't be aware of your subtle qualities. When you don't feel safe, your body produces stress hormones in preparation for fight or flight and it's hard to go peacefully inside. Choose a place in your imagination where you are safe from outside influences. This may be in any form you wish. When doing inner child work, it is often desirable to have the child go to his or her special hiding place. Most people remember a special childhood place. Two possibilities are a garden or a safe house.

The garden and the house are places that incorporate a representation of every aspect of the person—psychological, physical, intellectual, spiritual or other aspect that exists in any form. In these places you may make symbolical changes in your life. You may come here anytime. Make any imaginary changes you choose as often as necessary until they happen in your physical life. The choice of the place is a matter of what is right at the time. Many people enjoy gardening and the images of planting, weeding and pruning are good images for expressing intent. Other people are not as comfortable in the outdoors; a house may feel safer to them. In these places you may summon the best authorities on any subject for opinions or direction. You may call guides, allies, angels, dead relatives or any other image that suits you at the time. You may create as many helpers as you choose to keep the work going. You may use storehouses of spare body parts that can simply be snapped into place. You may have, use or create anything you choose in your sanctuary to serve you in anyway that you wish.

Another useful imagery technique is to create an image of the future the way you would like it to be. Move forward in time one year and witness how your life is if you make no changes and just continue living and thinking in the same way. Move five years into the future, ten years, fifteen years and then twenty years. Witness these potential futures from an outside or detached viewpoint, as if you were a neutral bystander. Now return to the present and create a different future. Experience a year from now as it would be if you did everything in your power to create the future that you want most. Step into the image and experience it as if it were real and happening right now. Move five years, ten years, fifteen years and twenty-five years into the future— experiencing it as it will be if you do everything you can to create the life you want.

You also may go to the past to make changes to affect the future. You might find it useful to return to a past trauma and change your belief about it and your relationship with it. For instance, say your father was an abusive alcoholic and constantly told you that you were worthless until you believed it. You may find it useful to return to the time when you accepted his judgment and change your mind and release this belief and the hold it has on your life now and in the future.

A useful guided meditation when working with a life challenge is *Homecoming* from John Bradshaw's book by the same name. In this meditative exercise you return to your childhood home and collect your infant self, your toddler self, your preschool self, your grade school self, your adolescent self and your teenage self. You tell your parents that from now on you are going to take over parenting these parts of yourself because you are the only one who can know the needs of your younger selves. Say goodbye to your parents and walk off into the sunset.

Another helpful guided meditation is from Virginia Satir called the *Parts Party*. Imagine yourself sitting in a theater alone. Raise the curtain and begin to bring out parts of yourself represented as a person. For example, you might represent the funny part as Lucille Ball and the kind part as Mother Teresa. You might represent the tyrannical part as Attila the Hun. Bring out five parts of yourself that you like and have them stand on the right-hand side of the stage. Bring out five parts of yourself that you do not like and have them stand on the left-hand side of the stage. Go up onto the stage and look closely at each part from all angles and change them anyway you choose. After you have made the desired changes, have the parts merge with your body until you have changed and integrated each part. Please, no violence against your role-playing parts. They need your acceptance and respect. They have already been wounded.

When using imagery, the more clearly and accurately you can represent your life challenge, the more effective your visualizations will be. It is very important to study everything you can about your life challenge. Of equal importance is to work with your medical support system to learn as much as possible about how your body works and how your life challenge exists with and inside your body. Medical people are the experts and can give you the clearest images of the dynamics of your body and your life challenge. They can help you to create a clear representation of your inner working with precision if you listen carefully and ask questions.

Remember that they are also human and could be wrong. You must use you own senses to find out if what they are telling you is accurate. If in doubt, get a second and third medical opinion.

When working with your life challenge, try seeing things from the larger view. It's easier to understand the ways your lifestyle contributes to maintaining or changing your life challenge if you consider how it relates to your family and friends. For example, it's easier to work with headaches if you know what triggers them. A headache may begin when your spouse, children or others begin talking about a certain subject. When you understand this dynamic cause and effect, you have the means to act to reduce your headaches. They become more than a tension and stabbing pain inside your head and you may now expand the experience of the tension and the pain to include the emotions, the beliefs and the previous trauma associated with the headaches. At some point it's likely you will find an action that will change the situation so you no longer get headaches or they will become milder and less frequent.

You also want to include other aspects related to your life challenge. Notice how your headaches exist in relation to yourself and others. Notice the tension in your muscles, nervous stomach, adrenaline rushes and other bodily signs of stress. The more you understand about your inner and outer world, the more likely you are to find the proper action leading to your ideal of health, whatever that may be. Knowing how your headaches work may not result in a cure, but it may give you a little more control over what triggers and supports your headaches. If you understand that breathing a certain kind of dust in your workplace causes your headaches, you may choose to wear a dust mask. While you haven't cured the potential for headaches, you have removed or lessened an immediate cause of your headaches.

As your imagery of your life challenge grows clearer,

you can actively and precisely direct your healing processes. We are such complex beings that we have no chance of ever discovering, let alone understanding, all the natural ways our bodies have of creating improved health. When using imagery, make up any way of working with your life challenge that you please and try it. It may not work, but chances are if you are able to find it in your imagination, it has a counterpart in reality.

Make the most accurate representation you can of the inside of your body where the life challenge exists. Using your inner senses, see it, hear it, feel it, smell it and taste it. Know it as intimately as possible. Following the pain is a reliable way to follow a life challenge through your life as a whole, including the world outside. If you follow the pain, it will reveal to you things that contribute to it—setting, emotion, nutrition, abuses and so on. Change anything that your innate guidance suggests. Adjust your intent and images as you go. Constant adjustments are necessary and only you can know what you're experiencing and what guidance is available to you.

Sometimes it is difficult to distinguish between innate guidance and wishful thinking. As you practice experiencing (living like a baby does before words and beliefs) on a preverbal level, you learn to catch increasingly subtle images and sensations. Innate guidance is a sensation and is as effortless as smelling. If you are struggling or trying too hard, you are probably using wishful thinking instead of sensations based on true insight. With practice you can learn to know the difference. If you have doubts, it's probably wishful thinking.

A comparison test may help you. Think of a time when you found some inner guidance. Represent this in anyway you choose. You may see, feel, hear, smell or taste it. What works for you is what is important. Notice how this past experience fits into and feels inside your body. Compare that past experience and proven guidance with anything you have doubts about. Now, make up a similar guidance. Notice how the experience of the made-up guidance is different from the real thing and how these compare with the guidance in question.

Notice how this present doubtful guidance fits into and feels in your body. Check it against other times when you had inner guidance. Experiencing is the only way to learn this. Practice always brings improvement.

Using imagery, you may work indirectly with your life challenge. When you represent your life challenge as a child and interact with the child to help it get its emotional needs met, you are working indirectly with the physical manifestations of your life challenge. You are changing the emotional environment in which it exists. You, also, may work directly with the physical aspects.

Working directly with the messages of bodily sensations is simple and effective. Start by getting comfortable and bringing your awareness inward. Just notice, without judgment, what you find inside. Bring your awareness to the most present pain. If you find no pain, bring your awareness to an irritation (a small pain). If you find no irritation, bring your awareness to an itch or a tension (a smaller pain). Enter your body as if you were a tiny scuba diver able to maneuver anywhere. You will find any tools, supplies or helpers you may need as you move through your body.

Bring your awareness to the first area of concern and probe it. Feel it with tiny inner fingers and listen to it with an inner ear. See it, taste it, smell it and intuit it. Massage it with tiny fingers if that feels right. Call in helpers to remove wastes or make bodily repairs. Stimulate the area with sound or heat. Soothe with color, tone, coolness or imagery. Use any pleasant sensory image you want. Add a theme song to keep the work happy. Supervise repair or remodeling. Use your imagination in any way that feels right. This is what imagery is, using your imagination.

Light

Working in the body with images of light is a powerful technique. Russian scientists have studied biophotons or light that each cell of a human body is believed to emit. These biophotons can be tuned to any measurable light frequency, thus, each cell of your body can use any color of light as a defense. An ultra violet light can be emitted to kill bacteria, a harsh red orange color to kill viruses and a honey-colored light to kill some anaerobic intestinal parasites. Biophotons can be emitted as a soft glow, a laser sharp beam or anything in between.

Light may be used periodically. For example, a hot white light might be imagined as burning the blood supply to a tumor to starve it. This image may be used for repairing a tear or cut, or cleaning a clogged artery. The image may be experienced as bright static electricity—like intense and focused sparks.

Light may be imagined as a constant glow that surrounds an area or organ. For example, in working with people that are HIV-positive, you might experience the bone marrow bathed deeply in a harsh red orange light that penetrates and kills the virus in the white blood cells. This light may be continued for as long as the image continues. White light is effective for pain control and for containing the spread of toxic organisms or substances.

CAUTION: *When using light in any form, always release excess colored light including white light from your body when you are finished!*

Your body will tell you how much of the light is excess. Trust it. White light, like any agent that relieves pain, also can mask it and hide the sensory feedback that may guide you to permanent relief of the pain.

In all PNI techniques the only reliable guide is your sensory feedback and the innate guidance that directs you in the use of this feedback. As a child, it took an accident or maybe intent to put your hand on a hot surface, but it took no prompting, thinking, intent or willpower to quickly remove your hand.

Innate guidance is also automatic or involuntary. You may come to a place of difficulty (like burning your hand) through curiosity or false belief, but the guidance away from the difficulty is always there. It sometimes takes extreme discomfort to get us to follow it. You can learn to trust that innate guidance to take you away from what is harmful and to take you toward that which is helpful and useful. This is the cybernetic nature of life.

The safest way to use light imagery in healing is always to start with an image of thin, crystal clear water. Using clear light involves no danger of masking or overloading. The image of adding a more intense clear light glow to your body, or in your body, allows for healing intent to begin working. While probing with and directing clear light, it's possible that you will feel the innate guidance to add the use of color. Let that guidance choose the color to use. When using color, always tune it to the exact right qualities for your use. Follow your innate guidance to find the exact right color and method of delivering that color. The right color may be different from the color you start with. Trust yourself. This will be the most direct and effective use of light imagery.

One method of choosing the color of light for you to use in a given situation is to bring your awareness to the working area and let that awareness grow. When you have a clear awareness of your current life challenge and you hold a clear intent in your mind to heal it, place a finger on your forehead and notice what color you sense. If you are working with a headache, you may see red. You may have a feeling that this red would be best delivered by pumping it through your blood. The next time you have a headache, even though it might feel the same, you might see yellow and have the urge to breathe it into your brain.

If you are working with intestinal parasites, (color has proven to be effective in treating parasites and yeast infections), you may be guided to soak your entire body in golden light. The next day you may feel that attacking the individual parasites with purple laser beams is the best method. Trust your urges and feelings. If you think you may be following wishful thinking, use a comparison test (see pages 122-123). Experiment with color and fine-tune it as you work.

Use colored light with breath or sound. Each sense or capacity you focus with helps your healing. The following exercise combines breath and movement with light and imagery. Each exercise is from the ancient Taoist system, Qigong. I offer these exercises only as a guide. The most effective use of any of these tools is what feels right to you.

Bone Marrow Cleansing

Stand comfortably with knees slightly bent and feet together. Take a moment to quiet your body and notice your breathing. Step aside with your right foot until your feet are shoulder width apart and toes pointed straight ahead. Relax and bend your knees slightly and rotate your pelvis forward slightly. As you inhale, allow your arms to float effortlessly upwards like wings until they reach shoulder height with palms facing outward. For just a moment, imagine your feet reaching to the center of the earth and your head reaching to the stars. Imagine your arms reaching out to infinity. Exhale and let your arms gently float down until they meet below the waist forming an upright bowl. Let your hands rise to your navel holding the bowl as you inhale. Turn your hands outward as they pass your navel and let them continue to rise until they form a bowl over your head with the palms pointing up.

For a moment, imagine you are a tree with roots reaching deep into the earth. Turn your palms toward the top of your head and while you exhale, imagine pushing white light through the top of your head from the palms of your hands. Push the light slowly through the center of your bones. As the light moves down through your body, imagine pushing dark wastes deep into the earth. Repeat three times and release the excess light.

A variation is to continue to expand the white light using the breath to intensify the light. With each breath, imagine your skeleton glowing brighter until the light begins to push dark wastes through the pores of your skin. Continue to push the wastes until white light shines from every pore. Release the excess colored light.

Organ Cleansing and Charging

Bone marrow and organ cleansing and charging are adapted from the teachings of Ken 'Bear Hawk' Cohen, a Taoist priest and Shamanistic healer. In the practice of Qigong, there are five reservoir organs of energy. They are called the five jewels: kidneys, liver, spleen, lungs and heart. These organs may be cleaned, charged and rejuvenated with colored light.

Get in a comfortable position with your back straight. Bring your awareness to the organ with which you are working, in this case the kidneys. The exercise is the same for each organ, only the colors differ. Imagine with each inhaling breath (through your nose) you bring a azure blue color into your kidneys and swish it around. With each exhaling breath you release the air, darkened with the wastes from the kidneys, through your mouth. Continue bringing in the blue and releasing the wastes using slow deep abdominal breaths until you release all the wastes and the color is pure and bright. Release the excess light.

Continue cleansing and charging each organ using pearl white for the lungs, topaz yellow for the spleen, emerald green for the liver, ruby red for the heart and azure blue for the kidneys.

The Birth Council Exercise

Stephen Levine tells a story about a three year old girl who asked repeatedly to be left alone with her newborn brother. Her parents were a little afraid, but after seeking advice they decided to allow their daughter to be with the baby as they listened over an intercom from another room. As they listened they heard the sound of the door closing. They heard the little girl walk over to the infant. They heard the little girl's voice say, "Baby, Baby, tell me about God, I'm forgetting."

I'd like to invite you now to move toward that innocence, to move back to your childhood. Moving through time as if it were a river. Moving backwards on this river, moving against the current. Going back through the different periods of your life. Moving through days, weeks, months, years. Going back, riding the river of time. Going back to childhood. Back to the time when things were simpler and truth was easier, where there was more potential in the world. Going back to the time when all was potential. Going back through school, grade school, possibly pre-school. Going back to the time of being a toddler, to a time when you could barely walk, back to a time of crawling. Going back to infancy, to a time when your muscles were so new that they hardly worked at all. Going back, past birth back into the womb, so safe here. In perfect communion with your mother. Perhaps feeling sad because she is sad or feeling joyful, because she feels joy. Going back, growing smaller and smaller . . . back . . . back . . . the sound of your mother's heart beating becoming dimmer and dimmer until it fades into silence. Going back now to conception. Going back to before conception, going back to your birth council. Going back, communicating with the beings of your birth council. I invite you to spend as much time with your council as you choose, asking all the questions that you choose, being open to the knowing of a part of your greater self.

Take all the time you want and when you're ready allow your eyes to open and your consciousness to return to the room around you.

I Am

This is an adaptation of a traditional Qigong exercise as taught by Ken 'Bear Hawk' Cohen.

I'd like to invite you to just bring your awareness to your feet. Begin to settle into your body. Begin to ground as described in the Grounding exercise (see page 7). Let your roots go deep into the earth, and as you do so begin to work on centering yourself in your body. Begin to bring your

awareness fully and squarely into your physical body.
Quickly take inventory of what's going on inside, starting
with your toes and moving upward. No need to do anything.
No judgment about anything just notice what's there. Bring
your awareness now to the space just in front of your spine
and there you'll find a column of light, a string of light that
vibrates and says *I am*. Not the little i of the ego, but the
big I of your greater self. Just bring your awareness into
that vibration, and let the string of light move right down
through your pelvic floor and connect with the center of the
earth. And let it move out the top of your head now and
connect with that place in the universe that has the healing
energy you need now; that has this healing energy available
for you.

Just tap into that place now, and let the column of light
grow larger within you, growing larger, moving right out
through your skin now, creating a shell of golden light
around you. Within this shell of golden light you're
protected from many things. This shell is always available
to you to use any time or place that you choose. Now, bring
the energy you're connected to, the healing energy that's
available for you, to that place inside where your life
challenge resides. And just allow that energy to flow right
through your life challenge into the earth allowing the
healing to take place as you're connected in this way. Take
as much time as you choose now to bathe your life challenge in this healing energy. And just observe without
needing to do anything, without needing to judge anything
or know how it works. Just allow this energy to go through
you washing away anything that is appropriate to release,
any toxic waste, just wash it away to the core of the earth
to be incinerated. And drawing upon that place that you've
connected with in the universe for the guidance to stay out
of your own way; the guidance to know what you need to

do to heal your life challenge. Take all the time you need or want now to work with your life challenge in this healing energy or light. When you're ready, just allow your eyes to open naturally and easily and return your awareness to the room around you.

Protecting Yourself

Everywhere you go you leave a measurable amount of your own body energy. The I Am exercise, with slight modification, may be used to prevent you from unwanted resonating with the energy of others. In the exercise, after the point where the connections to the earth and cosmos are completed and after the protective shell is formed, notice if there are holes in your egg where your energy flows outward or where outside energy flows in. Take inventory of all such leaks. You may have feelings or memories associated with these energy flows. Just notice what you find without the need to do anything about it. You may associate these leaks or flows with other people or situations. The source or nature of the leak or energy flow and what or who they are connected with are not important in this exercise. The only thing you need to be concerned with here is sealing the leaks and stopping the flows according to your own choice.

When you have located a leak, put your hand on the part of your body where the leak is occurring. Imagine a membrane like a soap bubble. Use you hand to smooth over the hole and seal it so it doesn't inward or outward. Continue sealing the holes until all you are aware of are repaired. You may then choose to contemplate the nature of the leaks and how the energy flows through them.

If you are aware of no energy leaks or flows, simply

allow your hand to move to a spot on your body. You can trust your hand to go to the right place. Push against your hand with your awareness for a few minutes then repeat.

Core of Energy

Get comfortable with your back straight. Bring your awareness to your breathing and begin to breathe deeply into your pelvic floor. Imagine a central core of intense energy rising through your pelvic floor and on up through the crown of your head. Feel this column of energy growing more intense with each breath. Begin to draw all wastes from your body into the core where you burn and release them as mist from the rising column. Continue until you find no more waste material to release. These wastes may be physical, emotional, energetic, spiritual or any other kind of toxin.

Unruffling

The following exercise in therapeutic touch helps you become more intimately aware of the energy aspects of your body. You also may learn to be aware of more of the subtleties of your life. This practice is called unruffling and is the most basic and easiest to learn healing technique.

Learning unruffling should, ideally, be done in groups of three. One person does the unruffling. One person receives and the third observes. Change roles until each person plays all three roles.

Begin with the grounding exercise. The person doing the unruffling imagines an invisible connection between his heart and the heart of the receiver. This is a very important step. It increases the sensory and energetic bonds that develop between the doer and the receiver and helps the unruffler become sensitive to the subtle physical and energetic shifts in the receiver. The intent of the unruffler also is very important. The heart to heart connection helps to keep the intent of the procedure clear.

The receiver lies down. You the unruffler, begin to move your hands toward the receiver's body from a distance of eight to ten feet. You notes any differences in the feel of space surrounding the receiver as you approach. At a distance of six to twelve inches the unruffler begins to probe the space surrounding the receiver. You sense for anything that feels different, keeping your hands moving at a slow steady pace. Moving them too slow or too fast or stopping decreases the sensitivity of your palms. You may sense heat or cold, tingling or soothing, rough or bumpy. You don't have to search for a right feeling. Any area that feels different from the surrounding area is an appropriate place to work. An area of different feeling usually relates to injuries, imbalance or disease in the physical body. If the receiver is uncomfortable or in pain, the area above the discomfort is a likely place to feel differences. Let your hands guide themselves by feel to the proper distance from the body to work. Now, begin to stroke the area, starting from the highest point of the body to the lowest point. For example if you're working on an elbow, you would begin each stroke above the elbow and move toward the wrist. Continue to smooth the energy layer until it feels the same as the surrounding areas. In practice you might move from one area to another until the entire area around the body feels consistent. For this exercise, you may choose to change places after unruffling a single area, depending on your interest and time limitations.

When working on yourself, you may use the hands of your soft body to unruffle, massage or balance any area of your body. If you have tension in your back, close your eyes and do the grounding exercise. Then imagine yourself standing behind yourself massaging your back in the right spot and in the right way. If you have a deep muscle pain or cramp, imagine reaching inside the muscle with your soft body hands and massaging it. The soft body isn't limited to the surface of your body. You can massage internal organs or between layers of muscles. You can use your soft body in any way your imagination allows. When using this technique, it is helpful to use imagery or sound. Imagining using your soft body to rehearse anything you want to learn or become better at will accelerate your mastery of whatever it is, including healing.

Grounding to the Opposite

Sit comfortably with your back straight and begin to ground. Begin to bring your soft body into alignment with your physical body. When you are sufficiently grounded, centered and present, begin to probe your body with your awareness. Notice that within your body there are many different feelings. You may find tension and relaxation. You may find pain and pleasure. You may find within your body the opposite of any feeling you find present. Within us exists the potential for all things. If you find joy inside, sorrow must be within as well. If you find pain, there must be the potential for ecstasy. They cannot exist separately.

Bring your awareness to your life challenge and experience the feelings, images, sounds, words, colors or whatever you find. You can trust anything that you find is exactly the right experience for the moment. Find a place or places in your body that has the opposite experiences and connect the two places with energetic roots. You may have the urge to use other imagery for connecting the areas or to add breath, color, light, sound or vibration to enhance the connection. Try whatever feels right for you. You can always adjust it or quit using it if it doesn't help.

For example, if you find a burning pain inside, you can scan your body until you find a place of coolness. The opposite is always there. Connect the place of coolness to the area of the burning pain. You may feel the urge to imagine a cool blue light connecting the places. Let these places blend. As a client said, "It's like introducing it (life challenge) to another part of the body so it can teach it how to be healthy."

Breath

Many cultures consider one's breath as life energy, healing energy, prana, chi, ki, or shakti. In Yoga the breath is central to all health, life and healing. The health benefits of deep breathing are obvious, but the breath is also a powerful envelope or tool for stimulating the healing process. Breathing exercises bring greater body awareness and increased mental clarity. Both aspects fortify the intent and awareness process.

Breathing Exercises

There are thousands of breathing techniques. Any exercise that allows you to safely increase your breathing rate is probably beneficial to your physical health and self-awareness, however there are medical reasons for some people to refrain from doing exercises that involve deep breathing. If you believe you might be such a person *consult your physician before doing this or any other breathing exercise.* Breathing can also be a powerful catalyst for moving old, stuck emotions. If you are emotionally unstable, I suggest you do deep breathing exercises only with the supervision of an appropriate teacher or therapist.

The following exercise is based on one taught by Chardin Bersto. Settle into a comfortable position either sitting or lying down, it makes no difference. I'd like you to notice how you breathe. How deeply are you breathing? Does your breath only move in your upper chest, in and out, or is it moving in your belly now as well? Or, are you breathing deep into your belly? Just notice where you are right at this moment. Notice the quality of your breathing as the air moves in and out through your sinuses, down the back of your throat into your lungs and back out again. And just allow your breathing to move a little deeper now into your belly . . . breathing just a little bit deeper now. Letting more air move in and out of your lungs. Allowing your breathing to drop a little deeper now moving toward your pelvic floor.

Imagine that attached to your tail bone and pubic bone are the handles of a bellows. Each time you inhale the handles of the bellows move apart, drawing air into your lungs. Just experience now how you operate the bellows, pulling the air deep into your lungs and into your belly, drawing it right down to your pelvic floor. And, squeezing it back out again with such ease and comfort . . . with no effort. Just experience the delicious life giving air as it flows in and out of your body. Inhaling deeply into your abdomen now. Deeper with each breath. And as you exhale begin to imagine that your breath moves up from your pelvic floor, up through your spine and out the top of your head cascading down around you in all directions, enveloping you in a cocoon of breath. Bringing the air deep in your lungs, exhaling it through the core of your body, out through the top of your head, cascading down around you and coming back up through the bottoms of your feet, through your pelvic floor, back up through the core of your body, through the top of your head in a continuous stream of breath. Flowing around you like a living shell of breath. Just take as much time as you like now to experience this cocoon of breath as it moves around you and through you, nurturing and protecting you. When you're ready, allow your awareness to gently return to the room around you.

Sound

Physicists say all matter contains the essential energy of the universe and is held in a solid state by sound vibration. Light exists in the energy matter continuum between energy and matter. All sound is energy. All light is energy and sound. All matter is energy, sound and light. All sound carries an innate rhythm and frequency. The rhythm and frequency create harmony or disharmony with the total external environment as well our internal environment. So, we have our own innate sounds and rhythms that interact internally and externally in a way of harmony or disharmony. We are supercomplex instruments playing in a symphony of life. This is a symphony of personal life, family life, extended family life, global life and spiritual life. Each symphony plays within a larger symphony on into infinity. In this sense, we are all master musicians. We have influence over the pulse and harmony of the universe.

We have an innate ability to use the therapeutic aspects of sound with our bodies constantly guiding us. When we have a headache, we may want to make an *ahhhh* or an *oooo* sound. These soothing vowel sounds massage the brain and inside of the head and neck. When you have a headache, you never want to make piercing *eeee* sounds. This may be a useful sound for constipation or breaking up other restrictions, but you would find it hard to even think these sounds when you have a splitting headache. Your body will guide you in the use of sound. Trust it.

PNI uses only self-generated sounds. There are many electronic sound devices available. These would probably be unnecessary. You can likely produce any sound necessary with little risk of this self-generated sound causing harm. The safety factor in using sound that you generate yourself is the fact that you can constantly monitor and control the sound according to what you feel in response to the sound.

If a sound feels good to your body, it is a safe bet that the particular sound at the present intensity is not harmful and probably beneficial. If it hurts to make a sound, stop making it. If you get overly jubilant, you may risk strained vocal chords, but this is probably not serious in the absence of any medical problem with your throat, vocal chords or other body parts involved in making sound.

Noxious sound bombards us daily with constant, subtle stress. There are sirens, trucks, airplanes, jackhammers, fluorescent light hum, refrigerators, screaming children and music we don't like. It's interesting that toxicity of a sound, in most cases, is how we feel about it. Studies show that the most healing music in hospitals is the music you like. Many adults find Mozart's music is soothing and healing, but they usually find heavy metal music to be irritating and a hindrance to healing. In adolescents the opposite is true. They tend to find adult music boring.

The sources of noxious sound are almost endless. We cancel this noise by a process similar to the inner workings of new, high-tech car mufflers. As the engine exhaust passes through the exhaust pipe, a tiny computer analyzes the sound and an opposing sound plays through tiny speakers in the exhaust pipe. The result is almost no exhaust noise. Similarly, we can drown out a noxious noise by humming a pleasant tune.

The work of French physician A. A. Tomatis suggests that most of the sound needed to maintain good listening or promote better healing is found in Gregorian chants and the filtered music of Mozart. His method makes use of the Electronic Ear which is a safe source of externally generated healing sound.

Toning

The easiest way to develop a sense of what sound does inside your body is an exercise called toning. To begin, you simply make any elongated vowel sound you want and see how it feels. Notice which parts of your body absorb or resonate with the sound. Notice which long tones soothe and which tones irritate. Spend five to ten minutes a day doing this exercise and you will soon find many new uses for self-generated sound. Be certain not to strain your vocal cords. You may find it more comfortable to practice while alone in a car or in the shower.

When working with sound, allow your body to guide you. Quiet yourself inside and become grounded. Bring your awareness to a life challenge. The life challenge may be anything, even something as small as a slightly tensed muscle. As you probe inside, you will find something to work on even if you can think of nothing that needs fixing. Allow whatever sound that occurs to come out. As you continue, the clarity of the life challenge (physical, emotional, belief and energetic) increases and the clarity of the sound quality increases. Like massaging a sore muscle, your sensory feedback guides you in all aspects.

Toning has been particularly useful in remapping neural pathways by stimulating a path from the area of bodily disorder to the brain. Toning does not overlook other forms of self-generated sound such as singing, whistling, chanting and hamboning. Using a musical instrument to sound your life challenge is also effective. Use whatever feels right for you. I learned this technique from Don Campbell, Director of the Institute of Music, Health and Education.

Cooperating with Your Medical Treatment

Unlimited ways exist for using PNI to intensify other healing treatments. A discussion of a few specific techniques for helping with, participating in or guiding these treatments follows. The techniques that are easiest for you likely will be the most useful.

The most common treatment a physician uses is medication in the form of a pill, liquid, salve or injection. The first thing to learn is the action of the medication. What does it do and how does it do it? What side effects may occur? What are the desired effects and why are they desirable? The more information you have the better, however, this information is of little use until translated into your experience. If a pill is relieving a headache by causing the blood vessels of the head to relax and expand allowing increased blood flow, it is helpful to follow the process from beginning to end. You might see and feel the pill as you decide that it is time to take it. Notice the feelings in your body and your emotional state as you put it in your mouth.

Has anything changed by your choice to take the pill or in the act of swallowing it?

Follow the pill as it dissolves and migrates into the blood stream. If one possible side effect of the medication is stomach irritation, protect it with something like a buttery coating. Or choose another way of protecting it like a vibrating sound to prevent the drug from touching the lining of your stomach. Follow the medication as it moves in just seconds through your blood into your brain. Notice how your body reacts to the pill as it breaks up and moves through your body. In any instance where you find an undesirable side effect, even if it isn't a listed side effect, do something to change it. Protect your body in whatever way you can. Add to the effects of the medication with other aids at your disposal such as relaxing, natural body chemicals, light, sound, breath, imagery or anything else that occurs to you at the time.

As you receive injections, you might relax and follow the needle while pretending that it easily and painlessly penetrates your skin and muscle. Pretend a hole opens to receive it. Then follow the liquid through your body, noticing reactions and directing resources to reduce side effects and increase its success.

If the intent of the medication is to kill an invading force, such as bacteria, imagine it destroying the bacteria. You may choose to kill the bacteria with sound and light along with the drug. You may choose to change the chemical setting so that the bacteria cannot survive or direct the offensive blood cells in an assault on the invaders. You may choose to protect the beneficial bacteria from the antibiotic. It is against some people's beliefs to use such violent images. If this is the case, you might use images of gathering up the bacteria and removing it unharmed. You must work within your reality. The scope of your reality will change as you choose to claim more self-awareness, self-respect and self-determination. This is a natural evolution of consciousness, but to be effective with this work you must start from your current beliefs.

If the intent of the medication is to change chemical or electrical imbalances, experience these changes happening as the drug reaches the target area of your body. Choose for the imbalances to change in the exact right way.

If the intent of the medication is to kill cells in the body, as with chemotherapy or radiation therapy, guide the drug or radiation to the targeted diseased cells. Shield the healthy cells, not allowing the chemical or radiation to penetrate them. You may choose to use images of pipelines, tanker trucks or aircraft to deliver the agent to the offending cells. Or, you may choose images of light pathways and sound barriers. Use any imagery that appeals to you.

You may use these techniques for participating in surgery or other medical procedures. You may choose to remain aware during surgery on some level and monitor the operation for signs of complications. Even under total anesthesia, some patients are aware of events in the operating room. You may use imagery to rehearse the operation including your choice to control blood flow, heart beat, respiration, blood pressure, or other aspects of your physiology.

While rehearsing, you might find it helpful to set the scene of the operation in your sanctuary rather than the hospital. This gives you an increased feeling of control. If your surgeon is cooperative, you may want to have him or her talk to you during the procedure and keep you informed about what your body needs at all times. It's also helpful to rehearse the operation with your surgeon or surgical nurse.

Imagine feeling and helping with each incision. Follow each procedure in your mind and body. Imagine stopping the flow of blood to the area of the operation. Prelive the entire operation, from leaving home and entering the hospital to the time of complete healing. This process helps to reduce fear and trauma associated with the surgery or treatment.

When working with an acupuncturist, bodyworker, chiropractor, physical therapist, physician, psychiatrist, psychotherapist or any other health care professional, have them tell you what they are doing. Have them explain how and why it is desirable to do what they are doing. You can make this work faster and easier if you participate. It may irritate the professionals at first, but they will soon understand that it makes their job much easier and the procedure more effective if you understand what they are doing and follow the work in your body. What you can do by choice may amaze both of you.

You can adapt these techniques to any situation. The images that occur when working with a life challenge are always the best. The images often change as they become increasingly fine tuned to your needs and circumstances.

Your mind will only supply images based on experience. This experience is often secondhand coming from other people. It's important to keep returning to the present. What is right today may be a waste of time tomorrow. The images that arise as a result of attending to the present experience of the life challenge should prove to be the most productive ones. Creativity, respect, gentleness and presence are essential to this work.

Chapter 8

Working with a Group with Mixed Life Challenges

The following material relates to a model group that lasted twelve weeks. Twelve people participated in the group. Their life challenges included: HIV-positive, two types of cancer, closed head injuries, chronic fatigue syndrome, endometriosis, lung disease that defied medical diagnosis, environmental illness, and chronic headaches.

During the first eight weeks, group members were not allowed to reveal their life challenges. At first there was some resistance to not telling the exact nature of the life challenges. There were comments about shame in hiding the challenge. Several members told of growing up in homes where keeping secrets prolonged the shame. Some members expressed doubt they could benefit from working on unspecified life challenges. Other members felt betrayed from the start by the secrecy. On the other hand, some members felt that by not revealing their life challenge they weren't limited by narrow, traditional beliefs. The HIV-positive members were relieved that they would not be shunned because of others' fear of AIDS. This allowed all members to treat each other with dignity instead of as diseases, syndromes or social outcasts.

The purpose of having the members withhold the exact nature of their life challenges was twofold: 1) to protect the dignity of the members with life challenges that were shunned socially; 2) to allow the members to approach their life challenges in a new way. This helped to create an environment in which they began to build a new model of their life challenges. The new model used their firsthand images and experiences of the life challenge. We compared it to a model based on observations by other healing professionals and measurements by medical technology.

We found that each member had worked in different ways, with limited success, to heal their life challenges based on a traditional medical model. Some had used other healing techniques and were suspicious of and even hostile toward traditional medical professionals and treatments. We urged all members to approach their doctors with a cooperative and curious attitude, but to reserve the right to decide what was and was not appropriate for them. Some members also had some reservations about the intent and methods used by myself and my co-therapist.

We designed this group to approach and work on healing from a personal model of the life challenge. We based the model on the sensory and internal self-experience of each member as well as the medical model. We stressed throughout the group that each member should gain as much knowledge of his or her life challenge on as many levels as possible. We supplied them with guidelines for questioning medical personnel to gain a replica of the life challenge on an intellectual, feeling and imagery basis. We urged them to learn about the workings of all body systems involved in the life challenge (see page 179). And, we encouraged them to see in their mind's eye all the internal workings of their unique life challenge. In the group we led them through exercises to create an emotional, energetic and tactile model of their unique life challenge. They explored the emotional aspects and dynamics of the life challenge within their family and social settings.

We encouraged members to relate to their life challenges as the problem child in a dysfunctional family. We did this so as not to blame their present life challenge on past family life. We emphasized that family rules or dynamics served to maintain the emotional and energetic balance of their worlds in ways that provided fertile ground for developing and maintaining different life challenges. As mentioned earlier, emotions are real and measurable electrochemical events. They affect your immune system, whether joy or depression, and may even be present as physical pain. Emotions and beliefs (or intent) affect all body functions and are necessary, working partners with your immune system.

In early groups, we had led members through exercises in which they imagined their present feelings as animals, plants or forces of nature. These images then interacted with the life challenges as other animals, plants or forces of nature using guided imagery. In later groups, members imagined the life challenge as an inner child that interacted both within and outside the family. Each member used the inner guidance from the exercises to shift their environment to a healthier one. They treated the pain or discomfort as a guide in the quest for a healthier mind, body and spirit. This guidance came as sensory imagery (the language of the subconscious mind) and as verbal direction or feelings.

To discover if pain is physical or emotional, you must go deeper. Psychological and spiritual pains have an emotional and physical pain as part of their expression. No difference exists on the physical level. The same neural circuitry handles emotional and physical pain impulses giving credit to the theory that the body and mind are not separate, but the same. We are much greater than we think.

After twelve weeks, most members were unwilling to
return to their old views. They felt that to do so limited them
in their abilities to heal. By using their personal images and
language, they found that they could affect their life challenges in ways previously unavailable to them. They began
to discover the broad aspects of the dynamics of their life
challenges. They found their families, friends, social and
work environments each played a part in the creation and
maintenance of their life challenge. They learned that to
truly heal themselves, including the bodily sensations of
their life challenges, they must make extended changes in
their beliefs and attitudes.

They found earlier beliefs and attitudes helped to maintain the setting in which their unique life challenges could
thrive. They transformed expectations of instant
miraculous cures into knowing that it takes time and careful
work to change one's beliefs and environment. They
needed time to set up new balances. They translated their
new beliefs into a holistic model. They used symbols and
language easily understood by each member. This is the
innate wisdom or guidance that we stressed throughout the
group as the key to finding the exact right treatment for each
member.

First Week

Week one of the group began with the business and
dynamics of the group. We discussed vibrant truth (inner
symbols) to help confirm how and in what form inner
guidance might come to each member. Everyone has a
unique way of seeing the world and themselves. We
stressed that the symbols, sensations or ideas that emerged
during the exercises would be the proper way (language)

to address the life challenge for that person. The person's language is the easiest framework for personal understanding. It's the language of the subconscious mind representing his or her sensory, neural and mental messages.

We discussed new age guilt—the popular idea that you create your reality and therefore any life challenge is of your choosing. Since you chose and create your life challenge, you can uncreate it. If you don't cure yourself, it must be because you are selfish or uncaring, or demand that someone else take responsibility for you. The guilt comes from being unable to uncreate your life challenge because you are lacking as a person. This is a little like taking responsibility for all the pollution on earth because you littered once. This view is wrong and has no place in the practical effort of finding personal healing.

We are not omnipotent. We are much too small to understand the larger meaning of our actions in the world. I believe we are part of the whole being of the universe and all that exists. We must have some role in the maintenance of this larger life system.

It's true you play a role in maintaining the dynamics of the environment that supports your life challenge. This support comes from beliefs, attitudes and emotions resulting from your upbringing and the way you experienced the world around you. You use the filter of those beliefs to mold your worldview. Your beliefs are sometimes like addictive habits that are very hard to change. As Barry Kaufman says, "Each person does the best they can according to their beliefs." You may have no idea how or when you acquired certain beliefs.

The rules you learned as a child were the rules of your family and society. These rules or beliefs became your reality. As someone in the group pointed out, "Your only responsibility for your life challenge is your ability to respond to it." You can choose to change the meaning of the rules or you can redefine any belief. For example, you might change the view of your life challenge from an unfair burden and source of constant misery to one of adventure and a chance to learn and grow as a person. You also can choose to step outside the rules or simply change the game. For instance, if you are in a bad relationship, you can leave, in essence, quitting the game. Or, you can change your actions in ways that cause the relationship to become healthier. The only guilt you have as a person is in not responding to your life challenge, but instead choosing to maintain it.

We asked each member to choose an animal that represented their self and the way they felt at the beginning of the group. For Jason it was a dolphin and for Sheri it was a duck. Later in the first week, we offered a guided meditation in which we invited the members to represent their life challenge as a different animal. Jason imagined his life challenge animal as a shark and Sheri imagined hers as a hawk. We instructed them to interact with the life challenge in its animal form as the animal that they had first chosen. The purpose was to begin to clarify the person's intent toward the life challenge. Your intent determines what if any effort is going to be made to heal. The options offered were to befriend the animal, to kill or devour it, to run away or hide from it, to try to scare it away or to ignore it. We also suggested they might find other ways to interact with the life challenge. The members formed groups of three to discuss the findings of the meditation.

The Unruffling exercise (see pages 132-134) followed. Members took turns approaching each other with palms extended to begin to feel the energy field that surrounds each of us. We tried unruffling each other's energy field to show that we could affect another person's field as well as our own.

Second Week

Week two began by checking in. As with the beginning of each session, the members were given time to talk about how the work and exercises they were learning was affecting them. We discussed the following topics:

- All exercises are very personal and cannot be done wrong. Whatever happens was the correct experience for that person even if it totally defied the instructions.
- Self-judgments were considered counterproductive. The intent of the group was to find individual healing. Judgment of and disrespect for oneself was discouraged.
- It is possible to monitor your intent toward yourself by noticing the way you treat others. As people, we treat others as we treat that part of ourselves that most closely resembles that person in the present situation. If you are treating another person with a lack of respect, it stems from your lack of self-respect. This disrespect is contrary to the healing process. Self-respect and self-acceptance are crucial to healing.

We asked each member to name a tree that reflected how they felt. In the meditation that followed we introduced them to the soft body concept. We lead them to realize that they could control the energy aspects of their bodies. We introduced the therapeutic touch theory that says energy and awareness are the same thing and that energy always moves with awareness. We invited them to relate to their life challenges as if they were forces of nature interacting with their chosen tree. Katie represented herself as a huge oak tree from her childhood days. The tree had fallen on her house during a storm and the house now represented her life challenge. We emphasized that no one really knows all their immune functions and urged them to use anything that came to mind.

Groups of four formed pairs for the next exercise. We told them to sit facing each other and to connect heart to heart using the soft body. The Power of Touch exercise (see pages 28-30) followed. We did these exercises so the members could become more aware of the subtle interactions with other people. We lead them to see how these interactions affected their emotional and physical responses to people and events.

Third Week

Week three began with a meditation focusing on the inner child as the life challenge. The inner child had the chance to state it's wants and needs. This was another way of representing the challenge as an ally or guide and of asking for its innate guidance.

We continued to explore the soft body through meditation. We defined the soft body as that aspect of life that was the difference between a living body and a corpse. The soft body infuses the physical body and brings life to it. The members noticed different ways in which they infused relationships, places, material possessions and ideas with their life energy.

The Where Does a Touch Begin exercise (see pages 30-31) followed bringing more awareness to the interaction of one's own soft body with the bodies of others.

Fourth Week

Week four began with everyone checking in. A meditation followed in which we asked members to again represent their life challenges as an inner child. We explored the tie between the child and its parents. We suggested that the child was trying to gain parental approval.

We used John Bradshaw's homecoming meditation from the book *Homecoming: Reclaiming and Championing Your Inner Child.* In this meditation the member imagines returning to their earlier home(s) to collect the infant, toddler, preschooler, grade-schooler and adolescent selves. They thanked their parents for doing the best they could and told them that from now on all parenting would be assumed by the grown-up self. Then they waved goodbye and left home.

The homecoming meditation proved to be meaningful for several members. The most stunning example was John, a man in his fifties, whose father had died when he was a small boy. John had a lung disease that had defied medical diagnosis. He had had surgery to remove part of one lung. John's doctor monitored his X-rays every month but still John had a spot on his lung that resisted treatment. In the meditation, he saw his father for the first time that he could remember and was able to speak to both of his dead parents. Later on, his dead parents spoke to John while he was soaking in his hot tub at home. He said it was like his parents were attached to him in some way that drained him of energy. After the meditation, he noted they were attached to him in a different way which no longer drained him. He could now talk with them in his mind's eye.

His father had died of an unidentified lung disease and his mother of pneumonia. The spot on his lung began to shrink immediately after he began talking with his dead parents and by the end of the twelfth week, the spot had shrunk by seventy-five percent. He told his doctor about his experiences—only to be rebuffed. The doctor stopped his treatment and told John to come in only for annual checkups. John knew his healing experience was a powerful and sacred event and to be dismissed as a kook by his doctor caused irreparable damage to their relationship. John felt justifiably insulted and hurt.

After most meditations, we gave the suggestion that the work begun during the meditation would continue in their dreams. By week four most of the members had experienced an increase in the number and intensity of dreams related to their life challenges.

Dreams are a valuable tool for insight into life challenges. They are a means of using PNI on a deep level of consciousness and may be the most powerful realm for working directly with your life challenge. You may work with lucid (semi-awake) dreaming or use messages offered by the dreamtime images and emotions. The language of dreams allows intent to be adjusted and expressed on a level of basic honesty and clarity. Dreams allow a preverbal communication with the self. It's like a child who has consciousness, images and self-communication before learning to speak. Next, we did an exercise for working with dreams (see pages 114-116).

An oversight on our part was not working more with these dreams. We initially planned some dream work, but we left it out because of the more immediate needs of the groups' members. It is common to feel body pain and emotional turmoil when doing personal growth work of any nature or undergoing healing treatments. A good metaphor for this process is an infected wound which needs to be cleaned to heal properly. The cleansing can be quite painful, but the wound will heal once it is cleaned. We decided the immediate need of the group was to gain the skills necessary to handle this burst of pain and emotion.

We, therefore, dropped the dream work and increased emphasis on grounding thus allowing the members to become stable enough to stay with the emotional and physical pain long enough to discover inner guidance.

The Qigong Bone Marrow Cleansing exercise followed next (see pages 126-127). HIV-positive members welcomed the bone marrow exercise. The biggest obstacle to treating HIV is that it hides in the white blood cells of the bone marrow. The virus reproduces inside the cell walls of the white blood cells and protects itself as it reproduces. Clarence, an HIV-positive member, imagined a harsh red-orange light inside his bone marrow. He pictured biophotons focused into laser sharp beams penetrating the infected white blood cells and killing the HIV enemy.

Fifth Week

Week five was the turning point in the relationship between the group members and the facilitators. This was also the point where more trust in fellow group members developed. Even members who had felt insulted and skeptical in the initial meetings found more confidence in the ideas and techniques presented. The practicality of the main theme, that you must rely on your own sensory signals in whatever form they come to you, appealed to most members. We summarized the week by saying, "You must take charge of your healing, because no one else can know the unique qualities of you and your life challenge."

Most of the group also had increasing personal discomfort at this point in the process. Memories of past abuse, neglect and abandonment surfaced. These came in dreams, flashbacks, and meditations. All members were choosing to experience the past traumas and trying to learn from them instead of running from them. They were more willing to take responsibility for finding their healing without the need to put judgments or conditions on it. They began to release the guilt associated with their life challenges. The group went on with the practical matter of healing according to their ideas of health. They found more willingness to relive past trauma and move through it. They chose to release blame and judgment as a practical matter, since both are obstacles to improving one's health.

We introduced the A Safe Place exercise (see pages 118-124) in week five. In their imagined garden or house, we suggested each member picture their life challenge as a child. We suggested that they name the child and follow it through the day and watch, without judgment, as the child interacted with family, friends and co-workers. We asked them to regress the child to infancy and then progress from infancy to old age as their life was currently going. Next, we told them to regress the child to an earlier age where they could have made choices that would have created a healthier present life. We suggested they progress forward in age again and notice how their futures unfolded in the new, healthier ways.

Then we suggested, they could experience their lives as if birth was a small distant point behind them. They were to extend a line from birth to the present. The location of the present was to be inside their torsos extending to the ground through their right leg with the future opening large and bright in front of them. We told them to adjust this image in any way that felt good. We then had them imagine a blackboard in their garden where they were to list limiting beliefs about their life challenge such as "this is incurable, I'm going to get worse," or "I'm being punished for past sins." Next, they erased the board as a symbolic releasing of these beliefs. Finally, we suggested they take time to love and honor themselves and their inner children before returning their awareness to the room.

Almost without exception, none of the members liked the blackboard in their gardens. As an alternative, we suggested another image of release. We used the image of a hot air balloon rising into the sky. The balloon carried whatever was to be released and disappeared into space or burst into flames. We told them to use whatever appealed to them.

We used timeline images going from infancy to old age so members could experience their lives as a single event. The members were told, "The way you represent the past and future in your mind and with your senses determines the way you experience these ideas. If you are a visual person, you may see the future as large and looming. If you are a touch person, you may feel the future as pressing in. If you are a hearing person, you may sense the future as loud and noisy. You will likely use a combination of these and other sensory representations of the future. If you experience your future as opening in front of you in a way that is appealing, you will feel good about your future, making it easier to move toward that future. With the looming, menacing future, you will likely waste a lot of energy trying to avoid the future."

We continued, "Your representations of the past affect you in a similar way. If you experience your past as heavy and resting on your shoulders, it will weigh you down and be a constant energy drain. If you represent your past as a firm road that supports you as you move through life, it will be a source of guidance and strength that serves you daily. The changes made in the regressing to infancy and progressing to old age enhance your ability to alter the meaning of the past and future. You can change it from obstacle to resource."

Sixth Week

Week six included a review of previous sessions. In the new material, we presented the idea of pain as an ally and guide. After a short time of relaxing and noticing the breath, we asked the members to bring their awareness to a specific pain. If they had no pain, we asked them to bring their awareness to a minor tension or a smaller pain. If they found no pain or tension, we instructed them to bring their awareness to an itch.

We suggested they bring their increasing awareness to the area selected without judgment or need to do anything but accept the pain or annoyance. Next, we told them to breathe into the pain, cleanse it with breath or use whatever imagery occurred to them. We began a weaning process as we shifted the need for direction in healing to a greater emphasis on finding a suitable guidance through their experiences. As the group progressed, each exercise required less direction.

Seventh Week

Week seven again included A Safe Place exercise where each member returned to his or her safe place. They accompanied the child through its life and noticed how the child viewed the world. As always, we suggested that any aspect of the member's life could be found in some symbolic form and that it could be interacted with if the member chose to do so.

Several of the members found that they were in the

garden with the child and they just wanted to play. They realized that they had ignored their own need to play. This unfilled need had caused a constant low level stress in their lives and been a continuous drain of their energy. The intent of this exercise was to allow the members to see things through more innocent eyes. The result was that each member experienced something that was important to them even if they did not follow the intent.

This is a good example of how inner guidance works. What each person needed at the moment had nothing to do with what we believed they needed. From the beginning the group was repeatedly given the reassurance that whatever they experienced was the only right thing to experience. We also tried to provide the freedom to do whatever seemed right at the time, even if that meant screaming. The members had come to a place where they could find what they needed despite instructions that would have taken them away from this place. This movement towards independence was crucial for the success of the group. It also helped to reinforce that answers are in whatever form they come to you.

Next, we presented the Letting Go of Tension exercise developed by Dr. Richard Shane. This is a simple exercise that can be done with only minimal practice. In this process you increase your discomfort enough to discover how you continue to maintain it. When you have worked through the layer of everyday stress, you may discover the root of the stress. You can then do whatever works to relieve the root stress. If you are interested in learning more about this process, see Integral Therapy Institute in Appendix D.

We felt this was an easy exercise to learn and one of the most effective stress-reducing techniques available. Many group members were in need of a simple way to bring more daily stability to their lives because of the increased turmoil caused by long-suppressed memories. This gave them a tool to work with their beliefs and emotions. To work on an energetic level, we offered them other tools, such as grounding, from Life Energy Fundamentals ® developed by Pamela and Jeff Krock.

Eighth Week

Week eight included meditative work with the soft, aware body. Starting from a point, we expanded awareness to the whole body; then expanded to the size of the room. The expansion continued through to the building, city, state, country, hemisphere, planet, solar system, galaxy and the universe. Next, they reversed the steps and went through smaller and smaller forms until reaching the smallest subatomic particle. Next, they progressed back to full body size. A firsthand experience of the soft body isn't limited to space and time (see the Expansion and Contraction exercise on pages 63-64).

We discussed the role of self-talk as a series of beliefs and intent toward the world. As children, when we pretend, we make a world we can act in and make sense of. We make choices and adopt attitudes that make perfect sense in our make-believe world. As adults, we use the same means to act in and make sense of our lives. We make choices everyday based on our self-talk. These choices determine the relationships, events, ideas and possessions which we infuse with our energy. Our choices either help or hinder dealing with our life challenges.

We introduced the use of color in this session. During meditation, we asked that each person begin to add color to each layer of their body energy starting at the skin and moving outward. We then led them through an exercise to bring color to help in healing their life challenge. Each member chose their color, tried and then adjusted it until it felt right. These were the only instructions given. Many members chose colors that matched those in Chapter 7.

Ninth Week

Week nine involved the Water exercise (see pages 21-24). The symbolic meaning of water is the awareness of the interconnected nature of all things on earth. Life energy (like water and air) flows through our bodies and is the same uninterrupted energy that flows through all things. We asked the members to experience the relationships, places, ideas, events and things they were attached to as if they were droplets of water connected to their bodies by small streams of water. They imagined that other people who infused these ideas into their life energy were also attached to the droplets by water jets from their bodies. The more people that attached themselves, the larger the droplets became. The more intense the attachments, the larger the jets became.

This is what Shamanistic healers call *loss of soul*. They believe these attachments are the main cause of disease. Shamanic healing does not address most modern diseases resulting from viral and bacterial infections. A Shamanistic healer might refer these diseases to a doctor of western medicine. Loss of soul, in modern terms, represents an underlying stress we all experience in our daily lives. Unrelenting stress affects the immune and other body functions and can result in serious diseases.

Next, we did the Toning exercise (see pages 139-140). Most members found toning to be instantly useful. Some immediately adopted toning as a major tool for dealing with their life challenges.

Tenth Week

Week ten included extensive work on breathing. The members learned to be acutely aware of the mechanics of breathing as we guided them into deeper and deeper abdominal breathing. They learned to breathe into and through their bodies. They created an image of being inside an egg of living breath. The breathing exercise brought increased awareness of the physical body and its subtle sensory messages. Breathing also helped bring increased awareness of the flow of energy through the human body and the individual's ability to control this flow. Several group members had dramatic releases of old, negative energy. They felt as if a massive weight had left their bodies.

During week ten, we learned that one of our members who had been absent from the group for four weeks wasn't expected to live more than six weeks. The reality of impending death brought increased concern and intent to heal to the group. The fear of death stunned some group members and brought them closer to each other. Our discomfort grew since neither the group nor the facilitators were allowed to talk with her. When we tried to call, a recorded message came on. She never returned our calls. Letters and cards were never answered.

Also, in week ten, we did the Core Energy exercise (see page 132). We invited the members to release anything harmful or negative into the intense core energy incinerator to be burned and released as a mist into the atmosphere.

Eleventh Week

Week eleven involved working with the beliefs that each member had about his or her life challenge. This exercise would have been more effective if we had spread it over several sessions, yet most members found it to be a powerful exercise. One member astutely pointed out that this should have been one of the first exercises. He would have liked to have discovered the beliefs held about life challenges in the beginning. This would have been a way of bringing into focus the intention toward the challenge.

Next, the members listed ten beliefs they had about their life challenge. Then they listed five ways that it was a hindrance in life and five ways it was a help.

Some beliefs about how the life challenge was a hindrance were:

"It causes me to hold back and not participate
   in life as much as I could."

"I can't eat what I want."

"It makes me tired."

"It doesn't hinder me in any way."

Some beliefs about the life challenge as an asset were:

"It protects me from abuse."

"People treat me with more kindness."

"I can get out of doing things I don't want to do."

"It makes me move slower and enjoy life more fully."

Then, they listed five things they wanted and how their life challenge affected those wants. We discussed belief as intent. Finally, the members split into groups of three and discussed their beliefs.

A meditative exercise followed where members examined the beliefs about their life challenge. Then they connected with the earth and imagined a shaft of light coming from outer space and enveloping them in a shield of light. We had them imagine that the light connected to a huge vacuum that sucked away harmful beliefs or anything else they felt no longer served them.

Twelfth Week

In the final week, we focused on feeling the pending loss of the group and taking more responsibility for individual healing. We did a short exercise to become more aware of the grief of this loss and other losses that had been experienced throughout life.

Then, we formed a healing circle. The members went through a brief Turning Inside-with-Awareness exercise to connect to the healing energies of the earth and the cosmos. They let this energy flow through them to the center of the circle. As more energy channeled in this way, more healing energy was available to the person channeling the energy. We directed the first energy toward the absent member who wasn't expected to live.

Each member had their turn in the center in which they received three minutes of channeled energy. We did a closing meditation and the group ended.

Private wrap-up sessions followed where members listed the toning, imagery and therapeutic touch exercises as most productive. Most members felt that the private sessions brought the techniques to an important intimate level.

The most amazing finding to me, as a therapist, was the fact that all members except one found that his or her life challenge was catalyzed by some childhood trauma. These traumas fell into one or more of the categories of abuse, neglect, or abandonment by parents. The abuse ran the gamut from brutal physical and sexual abuse to cold, passive withholding of affection. After twelve weeks of intense inner work, members found it easier to see how these early life traumas tied into their present life challenges.

Jean told the shocking story of when she was little how her father shook her so hard her head whipped back and forth like a coconut on a string. She had been sexually abused often and on some occasions her father became violent and shook her until she lost consciousness. Jean had severe headaches and repeated head injuries all her life.

Sarah related that her parents gave her little affection. She made up her own stories and on some nights, she would see and talk to angels. She revealed, "They knew when I had been talking to angels and on those nights they acted like I didn't exist. They were afraid of my visions."

Jeff spoke of emotional neglect. As a child he had all the things he wanted except intimacy and touch. This lack of childhood nourishment left him desperately trying to fill his emptiness in destructive ways. Jeff later became HIV-positive.

After all the group members told their stories, it was easy for them to see how these early root experiences helped lead to their current life challenges.

The following story shows that we can positively influence healing. One thing that makes it difficult for the body to protect itself from the eventual ravages of HIV is the virus enters and lives in the type of white blood cells that direct the attack on viruses.

Before week six, Jane had missed several sessions. She developed pneumocystis pneumonia, influenza and a bacterial infection in her lungs. Added to this was a flare-up of hepatitis. Her T-cell count dropped quickly and required her to take large doses of antibiotics. Due to her sudden crises, I went to her home to teach her techniques which I thought would be helpful.

We started with some inner child work to clear her immediate intent toward healing. Next, we worked on killing the flu virus with light and imagery. We imagined recharging and cleaning her liver with color, breath, sound and imagery to counteract the hepatitis. I directed her in moving and balancing the life energy in her body. Finally,

I did some gentle work on her back to relieve severe neck and back pain.

Within two days, her white blood cell count doubled and her fever left. Four weeks later everything cleared up except the pockets of infection in her lungs. She said her physician decided to inject antibiotics directly into the pockets of infection using a needle inserted through her rib cage. She told me that she did not want to endure that particular treatment. She asked me to help her heal the infection before her next visit to the doctor. We worked some more with light, color, sound and emotions. When I saw her a week later, she told me her doctor had taken her off antibiotics completely. Jane's MRI revealed only a slight tearing in her lung walls where the pockets of infection had been the week before. Her doctor decided the antibiotics weren't helping, but something she was doing was working for her.

Her next experience with pneumocystis pneumonia was much easier and she recovered more quickly. Jane took control of her healing. No longer does she feel that she is at the mercy of people she doesn't understand or at the mercy of people doing things to her that she doesn't understand. Her medical team is now her allies and her captains. Jane, however, is the Commander in Chief of her medical team.

The progress that members made in healing their life challenges during the twelve weeks varied from small to tremendous. While the examples are all anecdotal, the experiences of this group and people all over the world suggest that one of the most potent aspects in your personal healing process is, *you*.

The single thing that seems to be most influential in any healing treatment, from western medicine to faith healing, is your relationship with the treatment and the condition which you are treating. If you choose a treatment you have no confidence in and you believe that your condition is fatal in all cases, the treatment may not succeed. If you delude yourself by saying that your condition is not dangerous, even if you have cancer or heart disease, so treatment is not important, changes in lifestyle are not important, changes in relationships are not important, and all you have to do is think or pray it away, you will probably not survive. Maintaining life as usual and sprinkling it with a few pretty thoughts and feelings does not go far in healing. If on the other hand you are willing to honestly follow your inner guidance moment to moment, meet the challenges you present to yourself with non-judgment, and make appropriate changes in your relationships with yourself and your world, you have the potential to bring about healing in every aspect of your life.

The most important personal healing traits are self-respect, self-acceptance and forgiveness. Despite everything that has happened to you, see yourself as a loving and lovable person. You must accept who and what you are right now. Once you know where you are, who you are and what you have to work with, the only thing left is to begin your journey, one understanding step at a time.

You create your life from instant to instant with your thoughts, intentions, actions and relationships. In this sense, only the immediate *now* exists. If you act in the here and now with vigilant respect for yourself and all that exists around you, your life will have deeper meaning and more people will treat you with respect.

If you meet yourself with respect, you will guide yourself to healing. It all begins and ends with self-respect.

Carl Brahe

Workbook and Tapes

Healing on the Edge of Now - *Workbook.* This workbook provides a format to explore and record your discoveries as you claim your own healing powers. Chart your progress as you experience the power and wisdom of your greater self. Journal your insights and the other treasures you claim from the exercises included in *Healing on the Edge of Now*. Workbook - $12.95 + $3.00 shipping.

Healing on the Edge of Now - *Meditative Exercises.* A complete set of all the meditative exercises from *Healing on the Edge of Now* on audio cassettes. You are expertly lead through each exercise by Carl Brahe.
Two (90 minute) audio cassettes - $19.95 + $3.00 shipping.

Workbook and Tapes - $26.95 + $3.00 shipping.

Book, Workbook and Tapes - $36.95 + $3.00 shipping.

Please send check or money order to:
SunShine Press Publications
PO Box 333
Hygiene, CO 80533

Appendices

Appendix A

Music Suggestions

Background music to increase productivity and reduce fatigue.
1. Any music by Mozart
2. *Cosmic Classics* by Don Campbell
3. *Music for Airports* by Brian Eno
4. *Comfort Zone* by Steven Halpern
5. *Pianoscapes* by Micheal Jones
6. Pachebal's *Cannon in D*
7. *Rosa Mystica* by Therese Schroeder-Sheker

Music For Going Inward

1. *Angels* by Don Campbell
2. *Jeweled Horizons* by Joe Coe and Steve Windfield
3. *Spectrum Suite; Eastern Peace* by Steven Halpern
4. *Rosa Mystica* by Therese Schroeder-Sheker
5. Pachebal's *Cannon in D*

Appendix B

Reading Sources

Andreas, C. and S. *Heart of the Mind*. Moab, UT: Real People Press, 1989.

Bach, R. *Illusions*. New York: Delacourte, 1977.

Bahá'u'lláh *The Hidden Words*. Wilmette, IL: Bahá'í Publishing Trust, 1990.

Bandler, R. *Using Your Brain for a Change*. Moab, UT: Real People Press, 1985.

Bandler, R. and Grinder, J. *Frogs Into Princes*. Moab, UT: Real People Press, 1979.

Becker, R. O. and Selden, G. *The Body Electric*. New York: William Morrow, 1985.

Bradshaw, J. *Homecoming: Reclaiming and Championing The Inner Child*. New York: Bantam Books, 1990.

Cade, C.M. and Coxhead, N. *The Awakened Mind*. London: Element Books, 1979.

Campbell, D. G. *The Roar of Silence*. Wheaton, IL: Theosophical Publishing, 1989.

Campbell, D. *Sound Physician of the Future*. Wheaton, Illinois: Theosophical House, 1991.

David, W. *The Harmonics of Sound, Color and Vibration*. Marina Del Ray, CA: De Vorss and Company, 1980.

Dossey, L. *Beyond Illness*. Boulder, CO: Shambala, 1984.

Erickson, M. and Rossi, E. *Hypnotherapy*. New York: Irvington Publishers, 1979.

Erickson, M. *Healing In Hypnosis*. New York: Irvington Publishers, 1983.

Feng, Gia-Fu and English, J. *Lao Tsu - Tao Te Ching, A New Translation*. New York: Vintage Books, 1972.

Franklin, J. *Molecules of the Mind*. New York: Dell Books,1987.

Grof, S. *Beyond The Brain*. Albany: New York State University, 1985.

Gordon, R. *Your Healing Hands*. Berkeley: Wingbow Press, 1978.

Hay, L. *You Can Heal Your Life*. Santa Monica: Hayhouse, 1984.

Kaufman, B. N. *Happiness Is a Choice*.New York: Fawcett Columbine, 1991.

Kim, Ashida *Ninja Secrets of Invisibility*. New York: Berkley Books, 1983.

Kubler-Ross, E. *On Death and Dying*. New York: Macmillan Publishing, 1969.

Kurtz, R and Prestera, H. *The Body Reveals*. New York: Harper and Row, 1976.

Kurtz, R. *Body-Centered Psychotherapy*, *The Hakomi Method*. Mendicino, CA: Life Rhythm, 1990.

Levine, S. *Healing Into Life And Death*. New York: Doubleday, 1987.

Levine, S. *Who Dies?* New York: Doubleday, 1982.

Liberman, J. *Light Medicine of the Future*. Santa Fe, NM: Bear and Company, 1991.

Maltz, M. *Psycho-Psybernetics*. New York: Pocket Books, 1966.

Matthews-Simonton, S., Simonton, O.C. and Creighton, J. *Getting Well Again*.New York: Bantam,1986.

Minuchin, S. *Pschosomatic Families*. Cambridge, MA: Harvard University Press, 1978.

O'Hanlon, W. H. *Taproots*. Ontario: Penguin Press, 1987

Ostrander, S; Schroeder, L. *Psychic Discoveries Behind the Iron Curtain*. New York: Bantam Books, 1970.

Pierce, Joseph Chilton *Magical Child Matures*. New York: Bantam Books, 1985.

Ram Dass *The Only Dance There Is*. Garden City, NY: Doubleday, 1970.

Samuels, M. *Seeing with the Mind's Eye*. New York: Random House, 1975.

Satir, V. *Peoplemaking*. Palo Alto, CA: Science and Behaviour Books, 1972.

Siegel, B. *Love, Medicine and Miracles*. New York: Perennial Press, 1986.

Siegel, B. *Peace, Love and Healing*. New York: Perennial Press, 1989.

Shah, I. *Thinkers of the East*. New York: Doubleday, 1965.

Stevens, J. *Secrets of Shamanism*. New York: Avon Books, 1988.

Stinnett, N. and Defrain, J. *Secrets of a Strong Family*. New York: Berkley Books, 1985 .

Villolodo, A.; Krippner, S. *Healing States*. New York: Simon And Schuster, 1986.

Wallas, L. *Stories for the Third Ear*. New York: W. W. Norton, 1985.

Williamson, M. *A Return to Love*. New York: Harper-Collins, 1992.

Zi, N. *The Art of Breathing*. New York: Bantam, 1986.

Appendix C

Guidelines for Questioning Your Medical Support People about Your Life Challenge

The most important thing to remember when asking about your medical problems or life challenge is that you have the right to receive informed and understandable answers to your questions. There are no silly questions. The more you understand what is happening, the more equipped you are to deal with your medical or other life challenge. What appears to be a silly question, may save your life.

Your medical personnel are obligated to answer your questions. Don't let them intimidate you. Ask about anything and everything that you are curious or concerned about. If you feel your medical personnel are not cooperative, let them or someone above them know about it. If your complaints are not resolved to your satisfaction, then change doctors. You are trusting your life to the chosen medical support system. Your life is important!

Here are some suggestions for questions which you may want to ask—however, your own questions are the absolute best questions to ask:

- What is the medical name of my challenge?
- What does that mean in plain English?
- What is my body doing already to counter the harmful effects of the challenge?
- What would have to happen inside my body for me to be challenge free?
- How would these things look, sound and feel inside if I could go inside and observe?
- What body systems, i.e., cardiovascular, pulmonary, endocrine, is this challenge located in?

- How is it causing problems in this and other systems?
- How does this system work and how is it rebalancing itself to deal with the challenge?
- What exactly happens inside my body when I receive the treatment or therapy being prescribed?
- What happens in my body when I take my prescribed medications?
- What can I do to help my healing take place?

Ask for as many details to be described in as many different sensory modes as possible. Ask how it looks, smells, tastes, sounds and feels and any other way you can make a representation of your challenge. The more clearly and richly you are able to represent, in your own mind, the details of your challenge, the more successfully you will be able to use the techniques in this book.

There are many support organizations for different medical life challenges. Ask your medical support personnel for help in locating them.

Remember, ask anything you want about your life challenge and get an answer that you understand. *Your life may depend on it*!

Appendix D

Resources

To find a Hakomi Therapist or get information
about Hakomi training or workshops:
Hakomi Institute
PO Box 1873
Boulder, CO 80306
(303) 443-6209

Krock Institute
PO Box 1329
Conifer, CO 80433

For information on Integral Therapy contact:
Dr. Richard Shane
3958 Wonderland Hill Ave.
Boulder, CO 80303

For information on toning and other aspects of healing or
enhancing learning with the use of sound contact:
Don Campbell
Institute For Music Health And Education
PO Box 1244
Boulder, CO 80306

For information on Rocky Mountain healing retreats
and residential healing workshops contact:
Visions Retreat Center
PO Box 7323
Golden, CO 80403-0100

For information on training in Qigong, Tai Chi or
Shamanistic healing contact:
Ken Cohen
PO Box 234
Nederland, CO 80466

If you would like to be listed as a resource in future
printings contact:
SunShine Press Publications
PO Box 333
Hygiene, CO 80533

Index